# RETIRED

## WITH HUSBAND

Superwoman's New Challenge

# RETIRED
## WITH HUSBAND

### Superwoman's New Challenge

Mary Louise Floyd

VanderWyk & Burnham

Published by VanderWyk & Burnham
P.O. Box 2789, Acton, Massachusetts 01720

www.VandB.com

This book is available for quantity purchases. For information on bulk discounts, call 800-789-7916, write to Special Sales at the above address, or send an e-mail to info@VandB.com.

**Library of Congress Cataloging-in-Publication Data**
Floyd, Mary Louise, 1945-
  Retired with husband : superwoman's new challenge / Mary Louise Floyd.
     p. cm.
  Summary: "Written for baby-boomer "superwomen," who successfully combined career with family and now are nearing or newly in retirement. With humor and optimism, one of their own borrows from corporate reengineering strategy to propose a vision (with goals, objectives, strategies) for a successful retirement for both superwoman and her husband"—Provided by publisher.
  Includes bibliographical references and index.
  ISBN-13: 978-1-889242-26-2
  ISBN-10: 1-889242-26-8
  1. Retirement—United States.  2. Husbands—Retirement—United States.
3. Wives—Effect of husband's retirement on—United States.  4. Women—
Retirement—United States.  I. Title.
  HQ1062.F57 2006
  646.7'9—dc22
                                    2006006552
Manufactured in the United States of America
10 9 8 7 6 5 4 3 2 1

To Ethel, Myrl, and Joyce, extraordinary superwomen,
and
for my beloved Ed and Spencer

# Contents

# List of Challenges

### (Superwoman Confronts with Her Retired Husband)

# List of Strategies

## (Superwoman Uses to Meet Goals with Her Retired Husband)

# Preface

THE SOLDIERS WHO CAME "MARCHIN' HOME" after World War II created the baby boom that began in 1946. My dad's poor eyesight disqualified him for combat. His engineering degree, though, qualified him for teaching meteorology to B-29 pilots, while my mother, probably because she was college-educated, gave IQ tests at Bell Bomber where those planes were made. Obviously, they got a head start on sitting under the apple tree together, because I was born a year before the population surge that earned the baby-boom generation its name.

Nevertheless, I consider myself a baby-boom superwoman, that woman who proved she could be wife, mother, housekeeper, gardener, cook, family social chairperson, volunteer, *and* wage earner. Millions of us are now beginning our retirement. We do not intend to do it the way our predecessors did. Superwoman's voice says her generation's retirement marks the beginning of a long and healthy second adulthood with all the accumulated wisdom of first adulthood and opportunity never before presented to an entire generation.

The Superwoman psyche in this book is a proper noun and transparent because I write from my own experience. I am a retired educator living with my husband, a retired corporate attorney. Together we raised our Gen-X son. My first-adulthood bio includes earning two graduate degrees; studying and working both in the United States and in Europe; writing curricula for database research, for English and German language arts, and for English as a second language for the Japanese; conducting workshops for local and national colleagues; and publishing in professional journals and local newspapers. As Young Career Woman of Georgia in 1973, I spoke to groups of young women about career awareness and educational opportunities, and advocated the passage of the Equal Rights Amendment by lobbying state legislators and participating in televised debates. I am a member of the Smithsonian National Faculty and the Delta Kappa Gamma International Society for Educators. I was a "tennis mom" and an exchange-student host. My hobby is perennial gardening.

Since my retirement, I have been appointed to the board of Keep Atlanta Beautiful and elected president of an Atlanta garden club and vice president of my neighborhood's civic association. I am awakening a lifelong yet previously dormant passion for abstract painting. Most important, I have forged second-adulthood goals with my husband.

Maybe because we've conquered so much, we superwomen can't envision a life (or retirement) without new challenges. So my first retirement challenge to you, my superwoman reader, is to help your husband attain his second adulthood identity. Then, as a team, the frontier you conquer together will provide the opportunity to be part of a positive change unprecedented in human history: discovering the potential for productivity, creativity, and self-fulfillment during second adulthood in the twenty-first century.

In my book the Superwoman character also acknowledges her parents' generation, who enabled their daughters to aspire to all their sons aspired to. Now that we've set the pace for women in first adulthoods, we have an obligation to model for our children how to live second adulthoods that look at seeming obstacles as challenges, and how to seize opportunities for positive change and growth.

# Introduction

IF YOU THOUGHT BOOMERS GAVE UP cause-based protesting with Vietnam and the civil rights movement, just try telling them they're senior citizens. Haven't you heard of *real* age, man? The generation that refuses to grow old began turning sixty in 2006. But wait, that's not old. Not anymore. It's the start of this generation's second adulthood.

The year 2006 marked the beginning of an unprecedented social change: 3.4 million members of America's largest and most influential generation, the baby-boom generation, turned sixty and began the countdown to retirement. This number will accelerate until 2024, when all 77 million boomers will have followed. From the way our country is acting, you would think a great gray wave was about to engulf the American landscape and leave an outnumbered workforce struggling to support a nation of geriatric dependents.

The boom generation's retirement is the subject of studies by Health Services Research, the Congressional Budget Office, the Economic Policy Institute, the National Institute on Aging, AARP, Stanford University, and Cornell University. In many regards, the consensus is doom and gloom: this generation's retirement will bankrupt Social Security and Medicare, stagnate the nation's economic growth, create a skilled-labor shortage, and make health care unaffordable. Boomers, so the predictions go, will leave all this in their wake as they sell their financial assets and take to the road in their RVs, until they dead-end in assisted-living facilities or nursing homes paid for by the next generation.

Retiring Superwoman (capitalized as a persona in this book) has a different vision. She dismisses these prophecies because she knows outmoded assumptions are being used to predict the results of a demographic shift for which there is no precedent. Boomer men generally followed the same life's script as men a couple of generations ago. But where in these prophecies is the late-twentieth-century phenomenon, the woman who proved she could hold down many and diverse roles (wife, mother, housekeeper, gardener, cook, family social chairperson, volunteer) *and* be a full wage earner? Believe me, she won't be spending her retirement playing shuffleboard. Nor will her husband.

What the prophets of doom call the "boomer retirement time bomb," Superwoman sees as a starter's gun and mile-markers for meeting her new challenge: setting the pace with her boomer husband to redefine retirement and the human experience. With Superwoman as team leader, motivator, change agent, and coach (never boss), this husband-wife team will use corporate reengineering strategies (right out of the workplace they just left) to change their me-generation to their re-generation. In their first adulthood they had objectives-based plans to provide direction and achieve goals, using thoughtful strategies to overcome challenges in the new global marketplace. In their second adulthood they will find direction in another objectives-based plan, proposed here in Superwoman's get-it-done voice.

In *Retired with Husband,* I write as one of many retired superwomen, but I've done my research and mean to speak for and to the approximate 17.4 million superwomen of my generation, especially the first wave of 4 million superwomen born between 1946 and 1950, who are now poised for retirement with their boom-generation husbands. (These "partnership marriages" comprise 45 percent of my generation's marriages.) This book is an optimistic, go-for-it rebuttal to the doom-and-gloom forecasts about boomer retirement. Indeed, *Retired with Husband* intends to be an entertaining and ultimately inspiring blueprint for this large segment of our nation's largest generation. It is not about approaching the end of life; it is about approaching a new life. I see our sixtieth birthday as a defining moment for the country because boomers will begin redefining retirement and redefining the human experience.

As my Superwoman persona blazes the trail in this new frontier, she forges a lifestyle change for second adulthoods, which are blessed with unprecedented longevity and a mentality ripe and ready for new challenges. To her fellow retiring superwomen, she says, as I did, "Here's your new challenge. Lead the way!" To her retiring husband, she says, as I did, "Wait till you read what your wife has planned for *your* retirement!" To her Gen-X children and succeeding generations, she says, as I did, "Follow our precedent into the exciting new era of second adulthood!"

Part One describes the evolution of the superwoman icon in its unique historical and cultural context. Because retirement removed her from just one of her workplaces, Superwoman doesn't suffer from the same loss of identity and life's purpose felt by her husband. She looks at her retirement as a second chance at life, like reincarnation without the death part. After analyzing her husband's predicament, though, she realizes that her first task must be to convince him that he is not the boomer in winter, that he is going through a mere hiatus at the top of his game. Using corporate reengineering strategies, she devises a plan to help the couple achieve their second adulthood and enter an unprecedented new era of human existence. This plan begins with the couple's retirement *vision,* advanced in Part One.

The structure of the rest of the book is derived from the vision. Four long-term goals support the vision and make up Parts Two through Five. The four goals are to be a transition survivor (*Getting a new identity in real time*); to be the luckiest person in the world (*Giving and getting love*); to be all that you can be—and haven't been yet (*Reengineering your lifestyle*); and to be the starlight (*Setting the pace for twenty-first-century second adulthoods*). These four goals are reached through a total of ten objectives.

The goals and objectives are presented in chronological order as the couple restructure their lives to achieve the vision. As the goals and objectives are addressed, so are the challenges inherent in fulfilling them. These *challenge* sections (see list on page ix) reflect baby-boomer values that must be overcome before this generation can seize its second adulthood. As coach, Superwoman realizes that the transition may be especially difficult for her boomer husband, and therefore several challenges address issues from her husband's first adulthood: his identification with his job and several hardwired aspects of maleness that were nurtured—if not created—during his coming-of-age. Other challenges are parodies of boomer obsessions; still others are indictments of a zeitgeist created by boomers and characteristic of their generation.

From the challenges, Superwoman develops reengineering *strategies* that methodically lead to the accomplishment of the objectives and goals. The strategies, listed on page x, are as varied as those used in the reengineered workplace; some are presented as scenarios, some as skills assessments, and some as role-playing.

Part Two (*Goal: be a transition survivor*) begins with a discussion of the challenges husbands face in transitioning to retirement. Under Superwoman's leadership, her husband becomes a transition survivor by letting go of his job-based identity and creating a new identity in his real time of retirement. He accomplishes Objectives 1 and 2 (*Take charge of time* and *Conquer new territory*) by changing his formerly scheduled job time to self-structured retirement time, substituting home for office, and becoming half the home management team.

Part Three (*Goal: be the luckiest person in the world*) discusses the second goal husbands need to meet before they can move on to achieving their second adulthoods, and it involves giving and getting love. In achieving Objective 3 (*Listen with heart*), Superwoman's husband masters a skill that is the basis for a loving and lasting relationship with his wife. With her as change agent, hubby practices listening empathetically and responding with one of the four *A*'s: acknowledgment, affirmation, appreciation, affection. As the meat in the intergenerational sandwich, Superwoman's husband achieves Objective 4 (*Put the works in that "sandwich"*) by learning to anticipate his parents' future needs, to share in parental caregiving, to validate the lifestyle of his grown Gen-X children, and to help the two generations flanking him to connect with each other. He learns in achieving Objective 5 (*Go for the gold and silver*) how to enrich existing friendships and cultivate new ones. Here Superwoman calls in Aristotle as an outside consultant on the three levels of friendship. Her purpose is to motivate her husband to work toward the highest level of friendship.

In Part Four (*Goal: be all that you can be—and haven't been yet*) the couple make self-empowering lifestyle changes. With Superwoman as team leader in the pursuit of Objective 6 (*Learn from first adulthood*), they adopt a retirement wellness program based on common sense and sound medical and nutritional advice, not on the hype du jour, and they put fun back into exercise. Just in case diet and exercise don't reflect their inner boomer, they explore surgical and nonsurgical cosmetic procedures. Beginning with Objective 7 (*Move out of your comfort zone*) Superwoman addresses the retired couple's need for further purpose beyond the jobs they held in their first adulthoods. Here is where their second adulthood will begin to live down their generation's me-generation label. Through a role-playing strategy, Superwoman activates the retired couple's responsibilities to eradicate prejudice, commit to lifelong learning, and practice and teach the responsibility that comes with choice and with the privileges of American citizenship. In pursuing Objective 8 (*Find your giftedness*) the couple pursue the latent creativity unrealized in their first adulthoods. First, though, Superwoman has to convince her husband of his giftedness, which is waiting to be tapped, and of the possibility that his previous job(s) may not have been his life's magnum opus. She uses the multiple-intelligences paradigm, and the hypothesis that inter- and intrapersonal gifts develop with age, to motivate herself and her husband to manifest their innate gifts heretofore unrealized. She particularly urges some form of community service or volunteerism.

Finally, in Part Five (*Goal: be the starlight*), Superwoman brings her reengineering of boomer retirement full circle. With Objective 9 (*Redefine work—and retirement*) the problem to be solved is that her husband still can't find a retirement identity as fulfilling as his job-based identity. This section explores what opportunities may be presenting themselves if a worker shortage is indeed in our future because forty-six million Gen-Xers cannot replace seventy-seven million retired boomers. The ramifications of a skilled labor shortage in the near future give boomers the options of retiring, continuing to work, or combining the two. These options open up exciting new variations on the theme of wage earning and personal fulfillment. Never one to rest on her laurels, in Objective 10 (*Seize your re-generation*) Superwoman cautions us about that as well—to vigilantly seek self-improvement beyond our successful transition into second adulthood. Routine, even a new one, can become boring. She reminds us that this generation has eluded trend analysis at each of life's stages, always shaking up the status quo and leaving major change in its wake. The emergence of superwomen was one of these changes. They are the element unaccounted for in the doom-and-gloom predictions of the boom generation's retirement.

\*   \*   \*

Under her leadership, Superwoman and her husband are chart-
ing the new frontier of second adulthood—the opportunity to live
another adulthood of unprecedented possibilities. As they reengineer their second adulthood by conquering its challenges, they
redefine themselves and their generation. They are guided by
Superwoman's blueprint and their core values, which embrace
change as opportunity for growth, accept accountability for choices, and recognize the unique giftedness of every human being.
Like the Jedi Master Yoda, members of the re-generation will be
recognized for their wise and trusted counsel. They will have
learned how to use their force and how to empower their succes-
sors. They will earn the reputation of humanitarian as the concerned and mentoring generation. Ultimately they will change
forever what it means to live, retire, and age in modern America.

## Prepare Yourself

This book provides an insider's perspective of the Superwoman
persona so often maligned by critics. Superwoman personifies
the major social difference between the boom generation and
its predecessors. Yes, she did it all—and with aplomb. She *had*
to be a take-charge know-it-all to break all those glass ceilings
while still anchoring the home. But the ideological difference
between Superwoman and her critics is that she embraces
change as challenge and views it as an opportunity to move forward instead of clinging to the past. She admonishes the trend
analysts—who she assumes are mostly Gen-Xers—not to put a
"best if used by" label on her generation. Boomers are morph-
ing into their second adulthood. On behalf of her generation,
Superwoman's prevailing message is, "Baby, you ain't seen
nothin' yet!"

# PART ONE

# Superwoman Leads the Way!

## VISION
### BOOMERS WILL REDEFINE RETIREMENT AND THE HUMAN EXPERIENCE

FASTER THAN A SPEEDING *grocery cart. More powerful than a junior prom chaperone. Able to break glass ceilings in a single generation. She's a mother. She's a homemaker. She's a wage earner. Look! She's Superwoman, living with retired husband. She has changed the course of the twentieth century. Can she bend the direction of the twenty-first? You bet your kryptonite she can!*

Here it is, Superwoman: your new challenge. You've survived the barbs of childhood and adolescence; you've met the demands of motherhood, career, homemaking, and volunteerism. Now the first of your 17.4 million in number are approaching the next challenge. No, it's not old age (whatever that means anymore). No, it's not how you avoid looking like your mother (you're armed with all the remedies for that). And it certainly is not a dearth of purpose. You can't wait to dig your teeth into all that creativity you've put on the back burner while you tended to your children, career, homemaking . . . and, oh yes . . . husband, the one who's retired now, too. That's your new challenge, Superwoman: retirement with your boomer husband. You married him for better or for worse—and that includes retirement.

You don't intend to let this wonderful man, your life's partner, wither away on the back nine 24/7 while you take on a new life. Maybe you should design a plan to motivate your entire generation into commencing its new life—starting with your husband. You can be team leader, change agent, or coach (never boss), but your husband has to be part of the process.

Here's why. Since the industrial revolution, life expectancy has doubled. That means that two centuries ago you would have been dead by now, instead of having a whole third of your life ahead of you. Your golden years are no longer life's denouement as they were for your grandparents; these years present limitless opportunities for a second adulthood, and it begins now! Born between 1946 and 1964, your generation is 77 million strong, the biggest chunk of humanity ever to be born in the same time period. This doesn't count the 8.9 million adopted by the boom generation because they were born too late to qualify as part of author Tom Brokaw's "greatest generation," Americans who grew up during the Great Depression and who were old enough to fight in World War II. You are the first to retire in the twenty-first century. As the force behind late-twentieth-century partnership marriages, retired superwomen are uniquely equipped to lead the way. What you and your hubby do with your retired lives will set a new precedent and help to redefine the human experience.

You were the first generation of women educated for a career outside the home. In school your male counterparts accepted you as peers and partners and drinking buddies. Remember when your mother discovered that you had been drinking beer—beer!—the macho alcohol that symbolized coming-of-age initiation into *man*hood?

"Ladies don't drink *beer!*"

"But, Mom, I'm not a lady. I'm a woman! I can be a lady when I need to be."

Raising her disapproving eyebrow, your mother asked, "And what, pray tell, is the difference between a lady and a woman?"

Then you broke into your banner song, Helen Reddy's "I Am Woman." Gloria Steinem, Rosa Parks, and Billy Jean King were your heroes. You matured during the equal rights movement. You assimilated many of its values, embraced others, and trusted no one over thirty. Your parents' generation was so hopelessly out of it, like totally square. You watched your mother (contentedly, you thought) clean house, cook, raise you and your siblings, and entertain your father's boss and clients while your father was winning the bread. That was his job; your mother did everything else. Your husband was reared under this same scenario. But probably unlike your mother, you were educated for a career; and the last decades of the twentieth century recognized women's professional competency, so you went for it. Marriage, children, and home management—when they came along—no problem. "Mom did it; so can I," you said. You expected it of yourself—so did your husband. And your mom said, "Uh-huh, we'll see."

Your place in American history gave you opportunities to escape stereotyped gender roles, but you weren't distanced enough to break from culturally prescribed life scripts. (It's that cultural lag concept you studied in college sociology.) You were the tail wagging the dog, a Saint Bernard–sized dog. So you became that late-twentieth-century phenomenon called a superwoman, juggler of career, motherhood, and the myriad responsibilities of home management, while your life's partner followed the model of his breadwinning father, with all the rights and privileges that began with "Honey, I'm home!" As they say, you had it all. So you think now that you can take on retirement's glass ceiling? Not alone. You have a husband to bring along. This time it's *his* challenge, too.

## CHALLENGE
### A New Mix of Hearth, Home, and Husband

Because you've managed to work outside as well as inside the home, you have literally earned the right to your new unfettered state. Retirement, the world thinks, means throwing away the alarm clock, imbibing all the mass media you can stand, and lunching with the ladies. No way! Not for you! You want to create, contribute, motivate, recreate, move and groove to another level. You certainly don't bemoan the loss of your job-based identity, any more than you lamented becoming empty nested. You make this transition from career and child-focused home to retirement because you're still CEO of your home—you're still in charge. You still wield the power of daily decision making and long-term goal setting for that "other job" you've always had. Retirement has merely removed you from one of your workplaces. Now you're in the enviable position of having fifty more hours a week *and* retaining an anchoring identity with hearth and home.

Not so your spouse. He lost his identity when he retired. He also relinquished his power and status in the eyes of others. And he is keenly aware of his new predicament. In a word, he feels lost. Sure, he's proud of you, his children, his dog, his golf game, and what he accomplished professionally. But our species thrives on challenge—it makes us grow and keeps life interesting. If we don't have a challenge, we invent one. (Look at Donald Trump.) Your husband had the good fortune to marry Superwoman. He fell in love with you not because you were a good cook and a cute cheerleader, but because you were the whole package: attractive, witty, intelligent, and well educated. Your independence was part of your allure. Unlike his father, your husband sought a wife who would be his *partner* in the life you would carve out together. But remember the cultural lag? Your husband followed the model of his job-focused father, the man who took for granted his wife's homemaking.

The retirement transition is tough for your man because he no longer has the job that defined him, motivated him, rewarded him with pay, and gave him self-esteem and purpose. During the anticipation stage, the male misconception of retirement is that retirement is nothing but fun—nonstop, liberated bliss. But boomer men, as much as they may think retirement nirvana is a golf course every day, can't escape their need for daily purpose. So, what happens when you see the man you love floundering because he has earned himself a place out of the workforce? Before your mother can say, "Let him watch football or play with the computer all day while you finally enjoy life!"—look! It's Superwoman! She's helping her husband make the retirement transition so that they both can embrace the limitless opportunities awaiting them in their unprecedented long lives.

## STRATEGY
### Create a Vision for Engineering Your Second Adulthood

Why not apply those principles of corporate restructuring you were devoted to during the last couple of decades at work? You know, the survival skills you learned in order to avoid being downsized, reengineered, outsourced, delayered, one-minute managed, and TQM'd. Why couldn't they be applied to retirement? You don't want to be outsourced from what's happening. No, you want to *be* what's happening! Go ahead, use the buzzword: you can *reengineer* your life for its second adulthood.

Since jobs and kids are no longer the focus, you and your husband will have to think outside the careers and car pools that structured your first adulthoods. First, formulate a retirement vision for yourselves:

> We envision our retired lives to be an exciting second adulthood that presents unprecedented, limitless opportunities for our generation. We will positively adapt to change so that we can enjoy the challenges of the future, enrich our relationships, and appreciate our lives. We accept the obligations of discovering our unique gifts and of contributing positively to society. We will set the pace in redefining the human experience.

This vision statement can provide a philosophical framework for setting long-term goals and developing measurable objectives that incrementally achieve the goals.

There are no obstacles in the reengineering process, only challenges. Social analysts say these challenges reflect boomer values and shaped our first-adulthood behaviors. Some are values we inherited from our parents and their forebears; some are values we created in our post–World War II zeitgeist; and some are just hardwired male values. These are the challenges we must conquer to attain our second adulthoods, and we will. From these challenges, we can devise strategies for achieving our objectives, thereby meeting the exciting goals we set for our second adulthood. We need to remind the social analysts and historians that our generation is still becoming. When Superwoman gets her reengineering plan implemented and in full swing, maybe Tom Brokaw will write a history praising boomers.

The strength of this approach is that it works. It worked at work and it worked at home. It worked in achieving all those goals you set in your life's first adulthood, even if they weren't articulated as such. Remember? You had goals to pay off the mortgage, to imbue your children with the skills they need for life without you, to housebreak the puppy, to plant an herb garden, to run a half-marathon at forty, to run a 10 K at fifty. America is a goal-oriented society. That's how we've made it so far. Change is inevitable. Boomers know that. Just when you thought you were au courant with surge protectors, computers went wireless. Such is life. It's all about looking at change and apparent obstacles as challenges.

Retirement is a new beginning. Besides, boomers think old age starts after age seventy-nine—until they get there, of course. You're still growing; you have a whole second adulthood ahead. And Superwoman is leading the way.

# PART TWO

# Getting a New Identity in Real Time

## GOAL
### BE A TRANSITION SURVIVOR

RETIREMENT CALLS FOR TOASTS AND ROASTS and attempts at eloquence: "Freedom is the quintessential joy of retirement!" or "Retirement is freedom's quintessential joy!" or something like that. Whatever. Your husband hasn't been this excited since—you guessed it—the honeymoon. "This is what I've been working for all my life," he proclaims. (Gee, and you always assumed he'd been working for his wife and kids. Good thing your mother isn't here.) In addition to the company cake that reads, "I'm away from my desk—forever," there are the parties in his honor, plaques thanking him for his "dedicated service: 1974–2006," and cards saying, "Old lawyers don't retire, they just drop their briefs" and "New territory is just a green away." Then there is the new routine of daily tee times, punctuated with all the John Grishams he never had time to read. He's riding the wave of his life, he thinks, into a sparkling ocean of endless no-appointments.

After about a month or so of this hanging-ten stuff, your husband crashes. That sparkling ocean has chops and surges and, beyond that, endless nothingness. Before we have your surfer boy become the Ancient Mariner, there's a point here: for most boomer men, retirement just isn't what it's cracked up to be.

Your hubby begins pacing the hallway as if he's searching for something he can't find. (Remember, *free* can also mean "detached" or "unoccupied.") What he's trying to find is his new identity. When he sits in his recliner and stares at the wall, he sees his retirement plaque: To Robert, in Gratitude for His Dedicated Service: 1974–2006. "Oh, my God, it's my tombstone," he thinks in anguish. "I'm finished. I'm over. I'm done. I'm *retired*."

What's going on here?

## CHALLENGE
### He Is His Work

Time, habit, and post–World War II mores conditioned your husband to identify with his job. Perhaps he was one of the vanishing relics, a devoted one-employer employee, or maybe he weathered the tsunami of being downsized from one job to another—it makes no difference. He's part of the boomer milieu in which men are defined by their jobs. Sure, he is still husband, father, friend, and five-over-par golfer, but in his eyes, he has lost his defining persona.

Why is it so hard for men to go jobless? It has to do with time and space. Before this sounds like Einstein's famous theory or a sci-fi video game, keep in mind that Superwoman is analyzing the male psyche, a task complicated by the fact that men don't verbalize their feelings. But that's OK; you use your X-ray vision, what your husband calls your ESP (because men don't understand sensitivity beyond a certain level—a very low level). Anyway, when your husband realizes he's lost his space, called "the office," from which he exercised power and control and derived his identity, he feels bereft. Even if your husband's job involved traveling, or if his "office" was cyberspace, it was still his space, his sphere of influence. He held sway over this space, which he filled with his life's purpose for ten thousand days (call it ninety thousand hours!). In his psyche, a void has replaced this lost domain. No longer can he attach nine hours a day to the space that defined his purpose. The more your husband was a type A, workaholic, push-the-envelope boomer, the more acutely he feels this loss.

That's where you differ. Despite your career's end, you don't suffer from the loss of job-based identity because you always had your home as your domain as well. You were always CEO of the household, the decision maker, the one in control. When your husband participated in home management, it was at your initiation. Transition to retirement is easy for you because it means, initially at least, more time to devote to this domain. The term *superwoman* implies purview over multiple domains, hence one who has multiple identities.

The fact that our culture has endowed the married man with one identity—his job title—and the married woman with a composite of multiple titles is illustrated in the familiar set piece, the personal introduction. When we are introduced to a married man, among our first getting-to-know-one-another questions is, "What do you do?" Without the slightest hesitation the husband (and father) answers, "I'm a sales rep for so-and-so" or "I'm a corporate attorney for such-and-such." After being introduced to a married woman, we never ask, "What do you do?" Why? Because we know that today's married woman has many identities, and, more importantly, she does not define herself by her job title—even if she works outside the home. In such a culture, how does your retired husband respond when he is asked, "What do you do?" Invariably, he will answer, "I'm a *retired* accountant" or "I *was* a product manager." The point is, he still defines himself by his job—the job he's retired from.

Which leads to the second challenge in your husband's transition to his new identity. It's his infernal use of the past tense. Is he telling us something? There you go again with that ESP. It's obvious to Superwoman: he's stuck in the past tense of his former job-based identity. But help is on the way because you have a reengineering plan for your man. Before you devise the strategies for his new identification with space and time, it's necessary to examine why time is such a big deal for boomers.

## CHALLENGE
### Retirement Is Downtime

Let's face it. At the top of the list of reasons you retired was freedom from being scheduled from nine to five. It doesn't matter what position you held; you were controlled by a work schedule, chopped-up time slots that defined your workday for thirty years. Notice the use of the passive voice. You *were controlled by* time. Now you *have control* over what you do with your time. To play, play, play sounds great, but you can't escape your cultural heritage and late-twentieth-century conditioning to being scheduled. This is not to say that you have to immerse yourself in the multitasking hurly-burly you just escaped. However, the simple fact is that boomers who are used to being all that they can be in record-breaking time bites cannot be happy for long in a goalless, directionless existence, much less gain a new sense of self under these circumstances.

What makes the transition to retirement particularly problematic for boomers is that they are time-obsessed. The groundwork for this obsession was laid by the Puritans, to whose work ethic our generation ardently subscribed. This ethic taught us that it's sinful to waste time. Benjamin Franklin's aphorisms were reinforced by our Depression-era parents: "a stitch in time saves nine" and "lost time is never found again." Our grandparents' generation had absorbed the time-efficiency studies of Taylorism that were basic to the assembly line of mass production, which put our country in the lead in the industrialized world. We inherited the benefits and the burden. *Tempus fugit* was the first Latin phrase we learned, and its admonition still rings in our ears.

*Alice in Wonderland*'s White Rabbit implanted the subliminal message in our childhood psyches that we were growing up in a time-impoverished era that was always running late. Because pop culture mirrors our nation's values, the significance of time in the 1952 film *High Noon* is emblematic of our inner clock. In this motion picture, Gary Cooper's face provides an anguished backdrop as close-ups of clocks inexorably tick out the passage of time, hence Cooper's fate—and our fate, too, we felt. We've been trying to beat the clock ever since. As preteens we "rock[ed] around the clock"; while coming of age we tried to "put time in a bottle"; and as young adults we believed that only time could stop us: "Time won't let me." When Mick Jagger sang "Time Is on My Side" in 1964, he expressed our generation's attitude about controlling time. And sure enough, at age 63 he and his Rolling Stones played the halftime show at Super Bowl XL.

We became adults believing that faster is better. Why else might e-mail, fax machines, and overnight delivery be putting the U.S. Postal Service out of business? Why else do we opt for microwaving over baking? Why else have we grown impatient with Internet dial-up and now even with DSL? Why are we irritated with bar-code scanning and looking forward to RFID? In our childhood the new science of atomic physics was cutting edge as it measured in tenths of a second. Michael Johnson, by comparison, was measuring in milliseconds when he trained for the 1996 Olympics. At the close of the twentieth century, we reached the epoch of the nanosecond, a billionth of a second. A nanosecond is made comprehensible as the time it takes light (traveling at 186,282 miles per second) to travel one foot. And we can measure that!

Our awareness of time is reflected in our vernacular: real time, downtime, quality time. Our culture, moreover, treats time as a commodity: we consume time, save time, invest time, and kill time—all toward the ultimate aim of believing we control time. The unavoidable point is this: you and your husband are leaving a work culture that equated productivity with instantaneity. To be competent, you had to be mobile, wireless, voice activated, multi-platformed, hands-free, fiber optic, gigahertzed. To be down, gridlocked, or tarmacked was synonymous with failure. It was the survival of the fastest.

But there's a second meaning of downtime that applied only when you were working. It meant leisure time, a short reprieve from productivity to which you were returning tomorrow or after the weekend. Before retirement, your husband's downtime was his leisure time, which began with that familiar "Honey, I'm home!" During this brief freedom from his work schedule, he read the newspaper, enjoyed the meal you prepared, played golf, coached Little League, or participated in entertainment that you arranged with family or friends. But, remember, downtime carries that other meaning—in computerese—of nonproductive, thwarted-of-purpose time. All your husband has now, he thinks, is the nonproductive type of downtime because he is not returning to the office tomorrow. Now his real time and his downtime are one and the same, 24/7.

## OBJECTIVE 1

### Take Charge of Time

How is the harried product of a time-obsessed culture expected to enjoy a day filled with nothing but downtime? If Superwoman doesn't want her husband to feel tarmacked on the runway of his new life, she'll have to help him construct a new time identity. And why is she qualified for this? Because she never had after-work downtime. When she left her office for the day, she focused on her other jobs. Her time away from work was always prescribed by children's schedules, meal needs, parental obligations, household management. In short, she's accustomed to structuring her unscheduled time. Now that she has nine more hours a day of unscheduled time, structuring it comes naturally to her.

Structuring unscheduled time does not come naturally to Superwoman's spouse. So how does she move him from being controlled by a schedule that defined his daily purpose toward an unscheduled life in which *he* defines his purpose? Since time pervades all that we have done, all that we do today, and all that we hope to do with the rest of our lives, it behooves us to get a grip on it now. Superwoman must devise a strategic plan for her husband to take charge of time. Otherwise, he'll be wandering aimlessly through this marvelous epoch that offers more exciting opportunities than ever before in human history.

## STRATEGY
### Get a Calendar—Get Three Calendars

Get a calendar. The kind you write in. Sounds mundane, doesn't it? Well, it is. But there's something to be said for rendering purpose and direction out of a blank space. The blank space is your husband's day, his week, his future. His calendar is what he now *chooses* to make of his future. A calendar, therefore, is a tool that empowers your husband. With this tool he can achieve his new identity in the real time of his retirement.

Since the activities of your marital partnership now emanate from the home, you should have three calendars: one you share and one for each of you. Your joint calendar displays the year, a month at a time, with enough space for each day so that you and your husband can record obligations—oops, better to use the carryover workplace term *appointments*. This calendar should also have a space outside the month's grid for future reminders—oops, *long-term planning*—which later can be transferred—oops, *nailed down*—to specific days. On this calendar, record "appointments" such as your mother's eighty-fifth birthday, your friend's son's bar mitzvah, garden club meetings, your husband's and your cat's annual checkups, and spring maintenance for the air conditioner. These are demands on your time, just as business appointments used to be—news to hubby, who left all this to you while he was breadwinning all those years. These obligations are laid out on the shared calendar so that you both will know what *has* to be done and when. Then work from this shared calendar to your individual calendars.

The act of recording these appointments gives your husband control over his time. More important, he is structuring his day, week, month, year—the rest of his life. You're enabling your husband to substitute his pre-retirement schedule with a structure that clearly shows how much time—the good kind of downtime—he can give to his personal objectives for the day. Tell your husband to think of this calendar as the skeleton for his new retirement identity. It gives structure to disjointed, formless time. Your personal calendars can be no-tech, low-tech, or PDAs, as long as they're accessible and portable. In this planner, record what you have to or want to accomplish that day—even if it's just "play eighteen holes with Jim," "call Mother," and "grocery shop."

This simple device gives your husband the prerequisite resource—time—for new and enriching activities, which will form the beautiful flesh he'll put on the skeleton of his new identity. When Henry David Thoreau said, "Time is but the stream I go a-fishing in," don't think he was just fishing all day and indulging in the aimless pleasures of his solitude in that cabin he lived in on Walden Pond. He was writing a book. The stream is his metaphor for time, ever-moving time, and the fishing line is a metaphor for how he used time—his calendar, if you will. He was, after all, a writer of the Romantic period in American literature.

His milieu, which he helped create, called for nature metaphors like that. In today's milieu, he'd be using a BlackBerry.

## OBJECTIVE 2

## Conquer New Territory

Does hubby finally realize? While he was occupied with making the family fortune, you had two and a half jobs—your professional or volunteer career, the management of the home, and at least half of the child rearing. No, he probably doesn't realize. But console yourself with the fact that you did it and it was fulfilling— much more so than your mother's role was. Your children are on their own now. No more racing home from work to juggle dinner around after-school play rehearsals, soccer practice, science project deadlines, and PTA meetings. Weekly laundry is geometrically reduced to four loads a week, and you and your spouse *agree* on what's for dinner. Weekends are—alas—your own. Although you may nostalgically look back on driving lessons, piano lessons, tennis lessons, all-day varsity wrestling matches, sleepovers, and prom nights, you tell yourself, "Been there, done that—and with aplomb." Despite travel and other out-of-the-home activities that retirement offers, you both will spend more time in your home. And you will spend more time *together* in your home.

Start playing the Rocky Balboa music. Your hubby's in training for his resurgence. He's conquered time. Now he faces round two in getting a retirement identity: his new territory. The reengineering objective? To transfer his former power-and-control-giving space—his office—to new territory—his home. When he feels he controls this new territory, or at least his half, he will have put muscle and sinew on his new skeleton.

## CHALLENGE
### He Thinks Ownership of the Castle Means Simply Paying the Mortgage and Taxes

You've always had control of the home—its decor, inside and out; its organization; its food supply; its laboratories (the kitchen and the laundry room). Sure, your husband always had his private space, whether it was his recliner, library, computer room, or workshop. But these spaces were separate from—indeed, escapes from—the routine maintenance of the home that magically went on around him without his involvement, or his notice it seemed. When you worked, you scheduled laundry for Saturday morning, grocery shopping for Saturday afternoon, yard work for Sunday afternoon, and meal preparation daily. Cleaning was catch-as-catch-can, except for the kitchen, which had to be cleaned at least nightly after supper.

Why did you assume this responsibility, in addition to child rearing and your career? You inherited these responsibilities and pride in home management from your mother, who represented the last generation of American women for whom mixing motherhood and work outside the home was stigmatic. The routine household responsibilities relating to food, clothing, shelter, and family activities were always yours because you wanted to be all that you could be and everything your mother was, too. Now you reap the reward—no retirement adjustment for you. But now you also reap the unique responsibility of your retired Superwoman generation, which is to help your husband realize his new life's vision for retirement.

In you, your husband has had the best of both worlds; he has had a co–wage earner and a home manager. Child rearing was the joy you both shared, even though you assumed most of the responsibilities: transportation to and from activities, party planning, school volunteering, homework supervision, wardrobe consultation, teen crisis counseling, meal planning, nursing the sick. Now that you're both retired, and he has a hole in his schedule, or rather a hole in his day where his schedule used to be, it's time to share the routine household responsibilities that don't go away with retirement. What is significant to your husband's new space identity is that responsibility confers authority, and authority builds self-esteem. The home is said to be a man's castle, right? Well, this epoch in his life affords him the opportunity for ownership in a broader sense than paying the mortgage and property taxes. In short, you're ready to share the nest. Daily, weekly, monthly, and seasonal household obligations should be fit into your calendars so that what you have to do gets done and leaves time for what you *want* to do.

Keep your goal in mind: to help your husband assume a home-space identity to compensate for the office-space identity he lost. Reengineering strategy says this goal can be achieved if it is divided into performance objectives, that is, specific behaviors that are measurable and achievable. You can't carp or even cajole, and certainly not command. You have to *show how* and hope to engage his interest in half the household chores you've always assumed. Strategy is important.

## STRATEGY
### Implement Managerial Style Change

You can't just suddenly say one morning, "Honey, I'm going to show you how to do the laundry so that you can do it from now on. So pay attention." No, you need to use a principle that is axiomatic to learning: a new skill is learned best when it is linked to existing skills or when the learner feels *motivated* to learn an entirely new skill.

Given that the average superwoman always did the grocery shopping, cooking, cleaning, home organizing, laundry, and most of the yard work herself, you'll probably have to abandon the idea of linking the acquisition of these skills to others he has learned. Instead, you'll have to take the motivation approach. But, you ask, how do you motivate someone—especially your husband—to take on routine household tasks? Prepare an inspiring, go-for-the-gold motivational speech and use the managerial buzzwords he bought into a decade ago. Tell him to think of his home as the organization he just retired from. Then tell him the following:

- You want to transform your home's managerial style from its hierarchal leadership (your doing everything) to situation leadership and network management (his doing half).
- You want to empower him with the management of key home functions (cooking, cleaning, etc.), which will maximize productivity under his special expertise and which the home is eager to implement.
- An assessment of his skill potentials via test trials will reveal which household responsibilities can best be addressed with his expertise. You'll assume commensurate responsibilities, and you know that some responsibilities require teaming and some are best outsourced.
- He needn't feel threatened (you'll leave your mother out of this); as a crucial quality control item, no permanent changes will be made until the outcomes of the test trials are measured (against your specs, of course).
- Feedback will be timely, and processes will undergo cross-functional feedback.
- Most important, there will be a focus on process rather than product (if he wants to cook, you'll eat it, by golly, regardless of how it tastes); on results rather than inspection (you

will put up with the three-day-old uncleaned litter box if the cat will); on involvement at all levels rather than only those of his choosing (he can't choose all outdoor activities, especially in January); and on long-term commitment to continuous improvement (it may take a while longer to teach an old dog new tricks).

- Nothing is sacred (*that's* an understatement) to the house-hold organizational structure that has been in place for thirty-some years. Indeed, it *must* change to ensure growth and success in the new life ahead for both of you.
- The major objective is for him to find personal fulfillment in his new workplace.

The leadership in this home management reengineering falls to you, of course, the current CEO of the household. Let's face it. Your motives are twofold: First, you want your husband to have a new base of operations over which he feels control and from which he derives his new identity. If he can't sink his anchor in retirement waters, he won't feel comfortable exploring new horizons. Your second motive is selfish (yes, Superwoman may join the rest of the world's mere mortals and be a little selfish). If he doesn't take on some of the household responsibilities, they'll still fall to you, and you're ready to move on! In short, it profits both of you to reengineer home management. After he buys into this partnering, you can initiate the reengineering process. And—quick—before he gives you the new and improved weed whacker for your anniversary, you'd better get this transition process under way!

What are the specific skills needed by your husband to achieve the objective of conquering this new territory? They are the routine requirements of home management, commonly known as housework. Despite technology having simplified these tasks, the home remains the place where we address the human needs of food, clothing, and shelter. Under these categories fall the human tasks requisite to meet these needs. To wit, under *food* are the procurement and storage of groceries, and the meal planning and execution. Under *clothing* is laundry. Under *shelter* fall the cleaning and organization of the home and its yard. So, which of these tasks does hubby want to assume? To determine this, you can't mandate or assign, nor can you ask. He'll think you're trying to establish grounds for divorce. Remember the strategy in reengineering. You and he must first *assess* his skills and preferences so that he feels he's a contributing partner in the restructuring process. This will give both of you a feeling of ownership in the ultimate product, an efficiently run household you can both identify with. Give it time—at least a year. And don't make this assessment seem like a test. Keep a sense of humor, and make it fun! Read on.

### Test Trial
*There's More to a Grocery List Than*
*Stagg Chili and Beer*

Since food remains basic to life, logic dictates (Superwoman does not dictate) that grocery shopping is the first skill to assess. The male inclination is to go immediately when he needs something, such as Stagg chili or health bars (the ones that promise eternal virility), and then to amass these items so he won't run out of them in the event of nuclear holocaust. Perhaps he's thinking that if he goes to the grocery store this week, he won't have to go for another month. Or maybe he's regressing to his bachelor days when beer and peanut butter were the only staples a refrigerator needed.

Your husband has to learn that grocery shopping is not done on a whim. Its guide is the grocery list, the prerequisite planning tool to preparing the week's daily meal matrix of a protein, a carb, and something from the longer-wavelength half of the color spectrum (love those veggies). The list should be posted somewhere in the kitchen, and items are added as they need replenishment. If it surprises your newly retired husband that birthday cards, light bulbs, and houseplants can be purchased at the supermarket, then his training in this core operation of the home may take longer than you project. And if he doesn't know why the grocery store is called a supermarket, you've been overzealous about your former role in this partnership, even by Superwoman standards.

You must teach him the virtues of list making and eating leftovers—that is, what he bought last week. Leftovers have a bad rap from his parents' pre-microwave generation. When he realizes it's all about money, space, and planning, he'll catch on. Such a learning curve may be tough for your spouse, and in the short run it will seem easier and less painful for you to do it yourself, but think how that will play out for you in the long run. Do you really want to continue this chore solo now that you're both retired? If cooking and food shopping are your thing, fine. But Superwoman sacrificed her Saturday mornings for decades so that she could get this chore out of the way before her son's T-ball and her daughter's soccer practices. For the most part she hated this task that demanded at least two hours of her harried pre-retirement time per week.

## STRATEGY
### Learn from Homo erectus

If your husband thinks it's beneath his male dignity (read male chauvinism) to grocery shop, he's been the victim of too much proper care and feeding. And you know whose fault that is! In retirement "bringing home the bread" means just that—literally. Try inspiring him with a lesson from history, the current theory about human evolution. Consider it the link between prehistoric grocery shopping and the growth of the human brain.

About four and a half million years ago, a branch of our tree-dwelling predecessors decided to take up life in the grasslands of eastern Africa. Well, that was fine as long as the mother hominid could stay home to protect and nurture her babies while the father hominid went grocery shopping for the family. It didn't take long—just a little over two million years—for these men to learn that the women preferred the better breadwinners. The women mated with the men who walked upright enough to spot good food over the tall grass and carry these groceries back home, and they mated with the men who were clever enough to bring home the bacon along with FDA-approved selections of roots, seeds, nuts, and fruits. By this time these predecessors of ours were called *Homo erectus,* and the men had developed their enduring passion for tools. The women put up with the men's tool-making fetish because these tools made amenities for their homes, provided their families with fresh meat instead of leftover roadkill, and amused their men while they were not grocery shopping. In short, that's how we evolved to *Homo sapiens.*

If your husband is going to cut the mustard as half of the retired partnership in homemaking, he'd better grasp the meat of this retrospective on human evolution. Remind him that if he can't learn from history, he'll be doomed to repeat it. And he wouldn't want to go back to his *Homo erectus* days because that was the BC era, before computer. Why is it that men ignore the need for laundry detergent but never forget the bananas? Could it be archetypical behavior from their collective-unconscious *Homo erectus* period?

### Test Trial
*Even Boomer Males Can Microwave*

Who would've believed that the luxury of spontaneously eating out can get boring? But it does. Maybe this just goes to show that variety is the spice of retirement. Now you have the time and flexibility to make meal preparation fun and creative. Gone are the days of pleading with children to eat their cereal bars before the bus comes, while you are chugging your high-test caffeine and hoping that rush-hour traffic won't make you late to work. No longer are suppers manic attempts to get mouths fed and stomachs satisfied before homework. Your era of entreating that green is good, and pizza is reserved for Fridays is past. And finally, finally, no more scheduling suppertime around your late-working spouse's arrival or the need to get the meal out of the way before you both spend the evening catching up on what couldn't be completed at the office.

As you adjust your lives to the freedom gained by losing a prescribed mealtime schedule, remember that your husband is accustomed to the midday break from the office: eating a lunch that was prepared for him in a restaurant, café, or cafeteria. If he now expects you to assume that meal-preparation role, you will be assigning yourself to a new form of *servi*tude and, ultimately, making him dependent on you for midday sustenance. He's not your guest; he's your partner in your shared new adventure. Let him fix his own lunch. He'll learn—the sandwich meat is in the refrigerator; tuna, in the pantry. In this way, you both eat when you're hungry, thereby avoiding interruption of more meaningful pursuits. God forbid that lunch should become something you *both* schedule your day around. He took the vows, too: "For better or for worse" but not for lunch!

Really, only one meal a day, at most, needs to be ceremonious. Better suited for such is supper, as a reward for accomplishing so much during the day. Try convincing your husband of the privilege inherent in creating a meal that indulges all five senses, of the honor in producing the meal that symbolizes the denouement of the day. If you've been among the 30 percent of American women (mostly superwomen) who cook on the grill, it's time to give it over to hubby. This is a culinary art claimed to respond better to Y chromosomes anyway. It's something atavistic—invoking the cave days after the male successfully speared the woolly bison for his clan's sumptuous seven-day feast. Let him conquer again—let him take the raw meat out of the refrigerator and throw it to the fire. And, remember, always reinforce this behavior with enthusiastic praise, like "Oh, Honey, I can't believe you've been hiding this skill all these years!"

After his cooking confidence increases, encourage him to graduate to oven and stove top. Remind him that civilization has come from open hearth to microwave in just 140 years, and surely he remembers Nikita Khrushchev citing American appliances as tools of laziness in 1959, so cooking today can't be *very* demanding. Nevertheless, you have to introduce the process gradually. Don't expect him to undertake a sixteen-ingredient, four-step French recipe at first. Start with rice or grits—the instant variety—and then work up to his favorite Italian dish, lasagna, no doubt, or something else with lots of carbohydrates. At any rate, make it fun. Prepare the dish together the first time. Steel yourself for his disappointment when he learns that Italian sausage doesn't come precooked in patties; for his surprise when he learns that heated mozzarella, ricotta, and cottage cheeses have different textures as well as tastes; and for his amazement when he learns that pepper is not always ground—or black.

After this initiation, if he doesn't pick up the pans and get fired up with them, subtle coaxing may be necessary. Impart to him the fact that meal preparation is no longer the sole province of the woman, that you are now an anachronism. In the twenty-first century, wage-earning spouses share this responsibility. You were history's anomaly. You were a super-woman of the late twentieth century, a bygone era when daughters emulated their homemaker mothers *and* took on careers outside the home.

There remains, nevertheless, an obstacle to your husband's changing his behavior even though intellectually he accepts the Gen-X belief in sharing household responsibilities. And it's your fault. If you're Protestant, you can blame it on postwar thinking that predestined you to this fate; if you're Catholic, you can blame the pope's ideal of family life; if you're Hindu or Buddhist, you can blame your karma; if you're Jewish, you can always blame your mother. *You* conditioned your husband to expect having meals planned and prepared for him all those years.

Well, get over it. That was then; this is now. Retirement is all about change. Now you have to *de*condition him. Point out that most accomplished chefs are male and that the culinary arts are a field pursued by some of your children's sharpest male friends. Remind him that having a signature recipe is an earmark of the refined gentleman. Recall for him that his childhood hero, the epitome of 1950s masculinity, Dwight Eisenhower, popularized Eisenhower steak, that delicious dish slowly steeped in broth, bay leaf, and onion. Try to convince him that cooking is a skill in the repertoire of the retired baby-boomer Renaissance man.

If your husband doesn't take to cooking, it's most likely because he views it as a mystery (one of those feminine mystiques you can't surmount). Because he's never done it or because he's never tried, it seems magical to him that you can boil (pasta), sauté (shrimp), dice (tomatoes, scallions, portobello), toss (spring greens), bake (croissants), and simmer (basil-vegetable sauce) simultaneously and have everything come together—voilà—into a perfectly timed three-course meal. Well, it ain't magic. It's social and cultural conditioning, and it's the ability to multitask, which seems to be a cross-cortex physiological ability that most of the male species was denied. This is not to say that men can't compensate for this deficiency with a little practice. Think of what was said in the 1960s of women's innate abilities to be engineers—or astronauts!—that *they* overcame.

Since this is supposed to be a partnering exercise to increase the vitality of your future, you may have to concede that if he doesn't want to cook, he doesn't want to cook. And, after all, the proof is in the pudding, poached salmon, or stuffed potato. Perhaps his three nights a week to cook should be microwaving stuffed rigatoni and throwing the prewashed salad greens in a bowl. (Wonder what Nikita would say about that!) If he still doesn't take to meal preparation even on this level, just tell him that you're flat-out tired of cookin', that you've prepared more than 10,950 suppers in your marriage, and as simple as modern convenience food has made dinnertime, you don't want the daily responsibility any more. You've got better things to do in your second adulthood. From now on, it'll be eat out or bring in!

### Test Trial
*Only Four Loads a Week and No Multitasking*

While you and your husband are assessing his culinary inclinations, he should be introduced to another necessity of life that doesn't disappear with retirement: laundry.

## CHALLENGE
*Appliance Is a Girl Thing*

Despite the challenge acknowledged in the heading, perhaps the weekly laundry routine will appeal to him because it involves interaction with machines—big machines in the scheme of household appliances—and men like big machines. Laundering, moreover, is a series of definable tasks that are necessarily linked to one another sequentially. That is, these tasks do not require multitasking as cooking does. Besides, he's seen those ads on TV that portray men (from the virile to the geek, so surely your husband made an association somewhere in between) in wild bubble fights with long-haired young women scantily clad in spandex. Who cares if he's doing a little Freudian sublimating? At least he's taking this chore off your list.

Since the children left home, laundry has been geometrically reduced to four loads per week; nevertheless, this chore encumbers four hours with intermittent human attention. Teach your husband the sequence of subtasks:

- sorting articles by color and washing temperature;
- dispensing the washing detergent (bleach and the twenty-mule team are no longer necessary);
- setting the washer accordingly;
- making mental note of when the cycles are complete;
- popping the articles in the dryer;
- sorting, folding, and returning the clothes to their niches.

Sure, this is not a Herculean task, but it is routine housework and requires a weekly time commitment. Now that you're both retired, *whose* time?

(Would you believe that 10,500 American men are injured yearly doing domestic laundry? Must be those bubble fights.)

If neither the bubble-fight fantasy nor the big-machine approach entices your husband to laundry duty, perhaps he can develop an interest if he looks at it from a historical or, more precisely, material culture perspective. It might surprise him to learn that only two centuries separate him from an essential role in the household's production of clothing. Actually, the evolution of American laundry is responsible for the doctrine of separate spheres, that is, the ideology that man's place is the office or factory and woman's place is the home.

With the exception of spinning and sewing, eighteenth-century American *husbands* did everything else in the domestic production of clothing. They raised the sheep for wool or grew the flax for linen, sheared the sheep or harvested the flax, and then combed and carded, all before their wives spun this raw material into thread. Weaving the thread into fabric was also the man's job. It's no wonder that the spinning wheel was a symbol for the house-wife. As a matter of fact, skill in spinning was a prime accomplishment sought in a bride by pre–industrial revolution men. (This was before cheerleading.) It is significant to note, however, that the clothing fabrics of that time—leather, wool, linen—were rarely washed. They were cleaned by brushing. Hence, laundry, as subsequent generations called it, was not a notable household task until . . .

King Cotton. It was the introduction of cotton as the preferred material for clothing *because it was washable* that created laundry. With the industrial revolution's inventions of the spinning jenny (1770), power loom (1785), and cotton gin (1793), domestic production of cloth was gradually transferred to the factory—along with the husbands. Manufactured cloth, primarily cotton, increased the amount of clothing people were expected to own. (Remember Scarlett O'Hara's many sumptuous gowns?) This meant more items to be laundered. Not only that, cotton needed to be ironed! The domestic labor of women was dramatically increased, since women were now solely responsible for home management, whether they did all the labor themselves or whether they directed servants or slaves to do it. Tara and mint juleps notwithstanding, it's no wonder that cotton was king and not queen in the cotton-producing pre–Civil War South!

Not until the proliferation of appliance technology in the twentieth century—and really, for most American families, not until after World War II—was laundering less than a two-day task.

Monday was washday. Tuesday was for ironing. The scrub board and small tub sufficed for the small quantities of clothing that were washed. When cloth making became an American industry, the increased demand for clothing led to the backbreaking drudgery of schlepping heavy wet clothes through a manually operated wringer after "carrying heavy buckets of water from tap to stove and from stove to tub, repeatedly overturning the tubs and refilling them, as well as . . . scrubbing," carrying, and hanging the clothes on a line, as described by Ruth Cowan.

Postwar American affluence brought appliances, notably the automatic clothes washing machine and clothes dryer, into the middle-class home. Hence, the advertising industry and pop culture—since one is a function of the other in a capitalist society—created the Doris Day image of the American housewife you grew up with, an idealization of your mother. She was the devoted wife and mother, who, with the help of labor-saving appliances, could perform household maintenance in high heels and pretty dresses and then greet her adoring husband at the front door at 5 p.m. and reward him with embraces and an effortlessly prepared candlelit meal. This same Doris Day icon tucked her sweet, appreciative child into bed while she sang "Que Sera, Sera," which recounted our grandmothers' best aspirations for our mothers, to be "pretty" and "rich." The latter, it was implied, was accomplished by marrying the right man. In the meantime, your real mothers were realizing that there had to be something more to a woman's life than being pretty, working in the house all day, and enduring the ennui that 1950s society had sentenced them to. Maybe that's why your mother encouraged you to be educated for a career outside the home.

Boomers were the first generation to grow up with automatic clothes washing and drying machines in their homes. Indirectly, these appliances are one reason boomer women were able to contribute to the family income, attain the status of superwomen, and raise the nation's standard of living. Laundering has become the sole responsibility remaining in the home related to the basic need for clothing and textiles. Unless you're into sewing as a hobby, you are outsourcing the rest. You buy miracle-fabric clothing, no-iron sheets, and fine linens machine-stitched in China. And what you can't wash with water, or what you don't want to launder and iron, you outsource to a dry cleaner or laundry. Boomers' babies wore *disposable* diapers. From two hundred years ago, laundry's rank in household chores has come full circle. It's no big deal again. And now that your children, who used to change clothes five times a day, are doing their own laundry elsewhere, it *really* is no big deal. It may be time, though, to relinquish to your retired husband this four-hour weekly encumbrance—and remind him that he doesn't have to plant, raise, harvest, shear, card, comb, and weave any-more!

### Test Trial
*It's Better Than Viagra—Yard Machines*
*Amplify Testosterone*

Whether or not your husband decides to become a domestic Wolfgang Puck in the kitchen or to pretend he's bubble fighting with Angelina Jolie in the laundry room, there are other avenues for him to find the joie de vivre that time constraints used to pre-vent. All those years you were being Superwoman meant taking care of the yard, too. Yard work, which your mother-in-law calls your "gardening," was the catharsis that psychologically prepared you for Monday morning's challenges at work. Sunday afternoon from two to five was the only time you truly had to yourself dur-ing your child-rearing years. You stole this time without guilt because it was another way you could contribute to the family's well-being. After all, are not the grounds an extension of the home? And the home was your jurisdiction: its decor, its cleanliness, its order, its function. Naturally, you cared, too, what the yard looked like. So, you put out the pansies in October, the impatiens and begonias in April; you pruned, you raked, you watered, you fertilized, you designed; and you even did some hard-core digging and transplanting.

Ever since men moved from agrarianism to industrialism, the yard, as it came to be called after *pasture* and *field,* became a territory of ambiguous purview. The yard was no longer definably the man's because he wasn't raising crops and livestock for the family's livelihood anymore. When he moved his job to the factory and office, he still maintained a modicum of involvement with his vegetable garden, but more as a hobby. The woman was given authority over the aesthetics of the family property because the yard was considered part of her domestic domain. So, there you were, superwomen, on your weekends, while your husbands coached Little League or played golf.

If you were lucky, your husband was willing to wield the yard machines—the riding mower, the leaf blower, the gas-powered trimmer. What is it about men and machines? They must think that such power is an extension of themselves, an amplification of testosterone. Ask them to prune a shrub and they get out the gas-powered saw for that delicate azalea or fragile hydrangea. Are they ever willing to bend over and pluck a weed? No way.

If your preteen children got involved (teenagers, you remember, always had something better to do), it was your son who wanted to relieve Dad of his arduous tasks with machines. Your daughter, thankfully, stuck up her nose at such labor and declared that she would earn enough to have a yard-maintenance company do her yard someday. And she probably will!

There still remains, however, the thinking in your family that good ole Mom, who anchored the yard for decades, will continue to care for it in her retirement. After all, isn't it her primary extracurricular joy in life? Answer: No, not all by herself anymore.

It's time to acquaint your retired husband with the soul-nurturing satisfaction of working with nature. In the first year of your mutually shared retirement, introduce him to the seasonal requirements of the outdoor beauty he has taken for granted. Teach him the facts of yardwork life; namely:

- holly needs fertilizing in the late winter;
- the azaleas, hydrangeas, and rhododendrons are fertilized immediately after they bloom in the spring;
- old growth on ferns and perennials is cut away in winter;
- deciduous trees and shrubs are pruned in the spring;
- daylilies and phlox are divided in the fall;
- summer annuals are planted only after the last frost and winter annuals around the first frost;
- all old mulch is removed after the last frost and replaced with new mulch, but only after the plants have been fertilized beneath their drip lines and the ground has been gopher- and vole-proofed.

Wow! How can all this be in your head? Simply because it was part of your superwoman role, that's how.

### Test Trial
*Who Gives a Dust Bunny Anyway?*

OK, what's left of transferring your husband's control over his office to his purview at home? It's the routine maintenance of the home itself, aka housecleaning or housework (or wife work, as it was once called pejoratively). Because your husband always assumed that housecleaning was one of those arcane powers of the wife, he never gave it much thought.

To assess his skills in this key operation of home management, you'd better not wait for the teachable moment. It won't happen. Initiate the assessment with a polite request. Say to him, "Honey, please clean the bedroom," and see what he does. Will he change the bed linens, vacuum the carpet, empty the wastebasket, dust surfaces, throw away old magazines and newspapers, put books in bookshelves, and hang up clothes? It's unfair to expect the husband of a superwoman to have acquired all these skills—until now.

The housecleaning process may seem patently obvious to you, but remember, you've been doing it forever. To introduce this repertoire of tasks to your hitherto uninitiated husband, you may want to take the academic approach of defining subtasks. Explain that the umbrella term is *housecleaning,* but this term encompasses dozens of specific tasks. So what does the verb *to clean* mean to the empty-nested, retired, twenty-first-century household? According to *Webster's New Collegiate Dictionary* it means "to rid of dirt, pollution, or extraneous matter." Given that this definition of *clean* is pretty much standard for American culture, you and your husband will have to reach a consensus on what is dirt, what is pollution, and what is extraneous matter in your home's interior. If you rely on your senses, it's when it looks dirty, feels dirty, or smells polluted. Extraneous matter is anything no longer useful. When it accumulates, it's called *clutter.*

Once these definitions of what really needs to be cleaned are established, you can decide how often the cleaning should be done. Specifically, where does a housecleaning activity begin and end? What is essential and what is unessential? Where do you draw the line between what is necessary and what is compulsive? Martha Stewart wanted us all to feel guilty about not being compulsive, and you see where it got her! The ultimate lesson for your husband is this: if he can live with it, so can you—within the parameters *you* set for cleanliness (and you never set the bar too high). Besides, who gives a dust bunny anyway?

Certainly not Superwoman. You've had too many other demands on your time to develop a compulsion for excessive cleanliness. But there remains, nevertheless, an unavoidable minimum scope to this necessary aspect of civilized living. There's floor cleaning. If the kitchen is used as a food-preparation laboratory, its floor should be cleaned twice weekly; other floors can be ignored until dust bunnies and cat fur become bothersome. Rugs should be vacuumed biweekly. Given the American phobia of germs, bathrooms need to be sanitized once a week and the kitchen scoured after meals. Twice annually, upholstery should be vacuumed, windows cleaned, and silver and brass polished. Furniture should be dusted once a week. And then there are the things that need to be done when they need to be done, such as taking out the garbage and recycling, watering the houseplants, cleaning the litter box, and deciding what qualifies as extraneous enough to be donated or trashed.

### Test Trial
*If His Screen Is Full of Icons, His Life*
*Is Disorganized Clutter*

While you are assessing what's extraneous and what's not, be sure you consult with one another. Your husband may never forgive you for tossing out that old *Playboy* magazine you found in the attic. How did *you* know he was keeping it for the interview with Jimmy Carter confessing he had lusted in his heart? And if your husband decides he's going to clean out the garage (wonders never cease!), be sure to show him which paint cans contain the specially mixed Chinese red you use for the interior of the lighted cabinets. You never know when you might decide to illuminate the interior of another cabinet, or need to touch up a chipped area.

If your husband is a pack rat, though, you may have to exercise executive privilege to get rid of clutter. He may argue that if it can't be seen, it can't be clutter. Well, just tell him that you know a falling tree makes a noise even when no one is there to hear it. Clutter is clutter is clutter, as Gertrude Stein would have said if she had had a husband with a computer screen full of disorganized icons, every Web site he'd ever visited saved as a favorite, and thousands of undeleted messages in his inbox. Anything kept should be relevant to your lives today—unless it's an antique, whose outdatedness makes it valuable. Keeping irrelevant junk diminishes the significance of important, valuable items. (Come to think of it, it's probably better to let you decide what's junk and what's worth keeping.) Items you keep should be systematically organized so they are accessible to both of you.

Retirement's change of lifestyle is the time to reassess your wardrobes. Give those business power suits to the Gen-Xers! Wait, never mind. You can't endure one of those get-real glares again. Give the suits to charity.

Revisit filing cabinets. Your ability to accomplish any task or goal is directly related to your ability to find the right information at the right time. You can say that to each other, but don't try it as one of those lesson-teaching profundities with your children or grandchildren. They'll say, "Well, duh," and then they'll make some superior remark about how *they* don't remember pre-computer days like you relics, and what's a filing cabinet, anyway? Did you know that the average person spends 150 hours a year looking for misplaced information? Surely not Superwoman and her retired husband. Maybe after you two finish all this transition stuff, you can undertake converting all your files to CDs, or whatever the state-of-the-art format is when you finish sorting.

That's about it for routine housecleaning. If you discount yard work and food procurement and preparation, that's about an hour

and a half a day, or approximately ten hours a week. (Sound familiar? Yes, one eight- or nine-hour workday such as you just retired
from plus the hour or two dressing for success and commuting.)
Now that you're both on retirement's even playing field, you can
equitably share these time commitments. Each of you should give
five hours a week to the labors that sustain a household.
Outsource the core operations neither of you wants to assume.

### Embrace Twenty-First-Century Thinking
#### A Man's and a Woman's Place Is in the Home and the Boardroom

You've helped your husband get over his boomer social conditioning that said cooking, cleaning, and laundering threaten his masculinity. Now he will gain a new time-space identity emanating
from the home, where his contributions are necessary and valued
in the marital partnership. Now you both can make plans for
more significant things in the luxury of your retired time—just as
you always balanced the time constraints of your multiple superwoman roles.

This balancing taught you how to prioritize—and housecleaning always fell to the bottom of the list. Indeed, you never had the
time to be compulsive about housecleaning. Boomer women—
whether working outside the home or not—never complain about
housework being burdensome, because such complaints would
imply that they don't have anything more intellectual or creative
to do with their time. They may say they dislike housework or
have found ways to handle it, but they don't claim it as a burden.

The motto of our late-twentieth-century social order, "A
woman's place is in the home *and* the boardroom," implied that
our culture finally accepted women's dual and simultaneous positions. It also tacitly implied that a man's place remained where it
had been for two hundred years—in the boardroom or office, that

is, *not* in the home. Instead, a man's home remained his castle, replete with the servant surrogate: his wife (and co-wage earner in two-thirds of today's families), who cooked, laundered, and cleaned the castle. The basic unfairness of this arrangement is changing, though, because your male offspring, the echo-boomer generation, had to clean their rooms and bathrooms, fold and put away their laundry, and microwave their meals because Dad *and* Mom were both working late. They did not grow up in a home in which mother did everything for them. As a consequence, they have been groomed for partnership in home maintenance.

What is significant here is that you and other superwomen set the pace for viable options in women's life roles: to stay at home and be devoted mothers and homemakers or to take on the multiple roles of motherhood, homemaker, and wage earner—in either case without social stigma. Because you chose the latter, you're too non-nest goal-oriented now to redirect yourself to the traditional role of homemaker while your husband challenges the sand traps. Neither of you finds meaning in these choices. You both feel there is too much still to learn, to experience, and to contribute in your second adulthood.

Now that you have taken care of the prerequisite housekeeping details for the reengineered life ahead of you, your husband has let go of the notions that he is his work and that retirement is non-productive downtime. He has created a new identity in real time. As former CEO of the household, you've helped your husband restructure his time and space to accommodate his second adulthood. You and your husband are twenty-first-century explorers. Just as your eighteenth-century predecessors realized their continental destiny, you boomers have a new post-career frontier waiting for you to explore. This is to be your manifest destiny. And in the process, you will be changing your me-generation into your re-generation.

# PART THREE

# Giving and Getting Love

## GOAL
### BE THE LUCKIEST
### PERSON IN THE WORLD

ALBERT EINSTEIN IS POPULARLY PORTRAYED as that cool dude who did some heavy thinking. His legacy included philosophical musings as well as scientific research and mathematical proofs. Our kids and grandkids comprehend Einstein's physics better than they grasp his answer to the question *Why are we here?* With no mention of antigravity, black holes, or an exploding universe, the simplicity of his reply disappoints and eludes them. He said that we are here for other people.

And then there's Gregory Peck, or perhaps Atticus Finch—one and the same for the Gen-X group who read, relished, and revered this up-against-stupid-thinking hero of the 1960 novel *To Kill a Mockingbird.* Two years before he died, this film icon said he wanted to be remembered as a good husband, father, and grandfather.

Of course, twenty- and thirtysomethings don't get it—yet. But we do. We're further along the trail toward the pinnacle in grasping the answer to the question that's nagged the human species ever since we've been a species. Why *are* we here? We're like the Roman god Janus, who could look backward and forward at the same time. And, also like Janus, after whom the month of January got its name, retiring boomers represent a beginning. Think of it as getting a second chance at your life, like reincarnation with all the acquired wisdom of your first life but without the death part. Unfettered by job responsibilities, you now have the opportunity to reassess and strengthen your relationships with one another, with family, and with friends. The magic about giving this love to others is that you get more out of giving than receiving, which is something else *Homo sapiens* has known since acquiring the *sapiens* part.

Janus must have been a woman. Why is it that you're aware—and your husband's not— that he's missing out on giving and getting love? Why does he avoid intimate conversation with you? He's the meat in the intergenerational sandwich, right? Then why isn't he strengthening his connections with his parents and children? Sure, he's got the same loyal golf buddy, but why doesn't he enrich other friendships and seek new ones?

Don't give up on him! Don't say to yourself, "I'll let him spend the day with a book and his computer, but *I* need people. I'll find fulfillment in my relationships with others." You're Superwoman. You're part of a husband-wife team! In this next inning of the boomer retirement challenge, your coaching skills will get another good workout. Your goal is to help your husband realize that Barbra Streisand was right when she sang that people who need people are the luckiest people in the world. Getting and giving love is what it's all about. Your husband may not even realize yet that people need people. The most basic and meaningful way to get him moving along this path is through improving his communication skills.

## OBJECTIVE 3

### Listen with Heart
#### (What Partners Want)

Relationship experts say that working spouses engage in only half an hour of meaningful communication per week. Now, in retirement, with both of you released from your harried schedules and workplace identities, you have the time and share the living space for enriching your relationship through improved communication. Actually, you may not have noticed deficiencies in your rapport with your husband until now. When a couple is said to have divorced because of irreconcilable differences, that's just legalese for "the husband and wife weren't communicating." Your marriage is still intact because you and your husband *have* communicated effectively—at least so far. Your relationship has survived the most demanding decades of your marriage, and so surely, you think, you communicate well.

Think again. In your first years of marriage, you saw one another only briefly in the mornings and evenings, on weekends, and during escape-the-hectic-pace vacations. In between, your lives were controlled by jobs and studies. Your early days with each other were consumed by the necessities of house hunting, paying bills, painting the bedroom, and visiting parents. And then came the truest blessings of your marriage: your children. Your domestic lives became child-centered. The syntax of your discourse seemed exclusively built around the words *ear infection, team practice, report card, sleepover, allowance, birthday party, prom dress,* and *graduation.* You simply didn't have time to think about your relationship's needs, much less engage in mutually empathetic conversation. You were too busy being good parents. Obviously, you think, if your marriage could survive these demands, surely it will thrive in a job-free, empty-nested state.

Not necessarily. Although you've been married for decades, you and your spouse are getting to know one another, in many respects, for the first time. And, for the first time in your relationship, you are together 24/7. How, you wonder, could all those years have gone by without your knowing that he loathes the telephone, prefers sandals, and is too shy to initiate social interactions? How did you miss that he's really a morning person, obsessed with family security, and a visual learner? And what has he learned about you in retirement? He has learned that you need daily social contact (someone in addition to him), and at the same time you *relish* your morning solitude on the patio with coffee to plan your day. He has learned that in June your daylilies nourish you more than food. He has learned that you are trying to build a rapport with his mother that you never had with your own, and that you're an auditory learner. Such seemingly minor (but significant to your life together) aspects of your personalities emerge when you retire. They are indicative of your individuality—individuality that demands mutual respect, or at least a reciprocity of understanding.

The key to understanding one another's individuality is empathetic communication, the most significant factor in enduring marriages, or, for that matter, any enduring relationships. Much is said about the lack of empathetic communication nowadays because it is a major problem in our society. We simply don't listen to one another anymore. Before Superwoman applies a remedy to the problem at its grass roots (in this case, her inadequately communicating husband), it's helpful to examine how our generation created a culture that undermines intimate communication, which put us in the fix we're in with marriages that don't last.

## CHALLENGE
### Boomers Don't Listen

A long time ago in a galaxy far, far away, people communicated just fine without—

blogs

e-mails

chat rooms

cell phones

call waiting

instant messaging

Voice over Internet Protocol

That was the pre-digital era. The prequel to this era started around the time we were born. That's right—our generation spawned the very post–World War II technologies that subvert intimacy and erode our ability to listen, the most important element in communication. We've gained instant connectivity to all people at all times in all places. We have fragmented and overloaded our attention spans. In the process, we have lost the ability to listen.

It all began with television and the transistor radio. Significantly, 1946, the year of the boom generation's genesis, was the year TV networks began regular broadcasts. Our arrival, no doubt the headline story, was televised to the privileged 14,000 households that owned televisions with three channels. There are now 248 million TVs (one for every man, woman, and child over ten) and 1,937 broadcasting networks and stations. The meteoric rise of television contributed to the decline of radio as family entertainment, but it also *coincided* with the development of the transistor in 1947.

By 1950 four million American families owned a television, the invention that added the visual component to mass communication. By 1952 radio had bowed out of its golden age, yet by the early 1990s Americans nevertheless owned five times as many radios as they had in the 1950s. So why hadn't radios just sung, "Happy trails to you" and disappeared during their hostile takeover by the family screen? Because they became portable. Yes, portable—thanks to the transistor and batteries. Radio's new niche coincided with our generation's coming-of-age definition of self: got wheels, gotta move, gotta listen to *my* music.

In the mid-1950s Elvis Presley and Little Richard heralded not only a new genre of music but also the blending of two simultaneous appeals to the senses, the auditory and the visual. There they were, before our ears *and* eyes, on the *Ed Sullivan Show* and *American Bandstand.* Indeed, Elvis's provocative sexual gestures and Little Richard's flamboyant vigor were half the appeal of "Heartbreak Hotel" and "Tutti Frutti." And so this new entertainment medium carried the message into now thirty-three million television-centered homes: rock 'n' roll and TV were here to stay. In place of radio, family entertainment had become television, which required the viewer's ears and eyes both. Our ability to listen to each other had begun its deterioration.

Radio's portability made it personal entertainment, but for whom? These radios weren't broadcasting Edward R. Murrow and playing Glenn Miller. The transistor radio blaring its top ten became emblematic of the boomer generation. Because radio was personal *and* portable, it became background accompaniment to other boomer activities—all our activities. So this morphed medium delivered its new message: "Just sit and listen? I'm portable, for goodness sake! Take me with you wherever you go!" We boomers now ask ourselves whether Ray Charles was like the blind seer Tiresias when he sang "What'd I Say?" in 1959. With its refrain repeatedly demanding, "Tell me what'd I say," was he prophesying the inability to attend to listening in the 1960s?

By 1980 CNN, with its around-the-clock, worldwide cable news-as-it-happens, eventually conceived yet a third demand on our senses as we watched and listened: the ribbon of late-breaking events at the bottom of the screen, which we feel obligated to read to be fully informed about what's going on in the world. And lest we miss anything, there is also subscreen text of the world's weather, Wall Street's activities, and the latest sports stats. Attend to listening? Only when we choose it from the smorgasbord of communication options offered. And then, of course, we mentally surf from one mode of news delivery to another, just as we surf the Web, scanning with our ears to the audio and our eyes to the video or the subscreen text. The idea is to get the essence fast, just as we use the Internet. On average, we click beyond a Web site's home page only 40 percent of the time. We know we are proficient twenty-first-century beings because we can listen, look at video, and read at the same time. If we can't get the message in a couple of seconds, we move on.

Blamed for our national attention deficit, commercial breaks command seven to twelve minutes per thirty-minute program and actively disrupt any attention we might otherwise sustain. It's no wonder we're too impatient to listen to friends—or spouses—as they grope (now defined as taking more than a few nanoseconds) for words to express feelings. We've been conditioned to think, "I want it fast and loud and state of the art; otherwise you've lost me. Sorry, it's time for a commercial. I'm tuning you out. Something else has caught my attention."

In the meantime, telephone technology—ironically advertised as the means to "reach out and touch someone"—has impersonalized our relationships and eroded our ability to communicate meaningfully. Examine a typical morning. You steel yourself for the hour it will take to make an appointment for a cable television technician to diagnose the fuzz on channels 44–78. You dial and get the inevitable staccato message: "This line is busy. For a charge of ninety cents we will continue to try the number for you during the next thirty minutes. You will be notified by a special ring and automatically connected once the number becomes available. To accept, press 1 . . ." So you carry the portable phone around the house, or pocket your cell phone for the day. Heaven forbid you get stuck on a landline! When the automated queue finally moves your call to the top, the cable company's recorded message informs you, "All technicians are currently assisting other customers. Your call is very important to us." Yeah, right. But that robot who's talking to you tells you to select from a menu of 1–8 to describe your problem, enter your zip code and phone number, and wait for a technician, who will call you within the next four hours. This sort of scenario has conditioned you to anticipate that your communicated need will not be fulfilled. It reinforces what you feel: no one wants to listen to you. And if you do get a live voice, it belongs to someone in India. Does he really care about your needs half a planet away?

And how about casual calls to friends—*friends,* mind you! How often do you have to leave recorded messages? Don't you sometimes suspect that friends aren't pressing "TALK" because their caller ID has identified you? And when a friend does pick up, how often is your conversation interrupted with call waiting or a second line ringing, which, you can't help but feel, is more important to your friend than your desire to communicate? As a consequence, you feel you are intruding on a friend's time if you consume more than a minute or two. So go your thwarted attempts to "reach out and touch someone."

In this digital era, telephones have become a means of contacting one another under exigent circumstances, or, at best, for brief, superficial contact while we are occupied—or preoccupied—with another activity. The newest culprit? The ubiquitous cell phone. If you're not among the 200 million Americans who own at least one, you're considered a pre-1990 enemy of modern convenience, an alien in the digital world. After all, why waste time just grocery shopping, watching a tennis match, or walking in the park when you could also be calling friends, checking on your parents, or placing a buy order with your stockbroker? Cellular technology has convinced you that you need a phone at all times and in all places: in the theater, on alpine slopes, in Carlsbad Caverns, rafting the Colorado, walking through the Alhambra. You can even check your e-mail in the Alhambra or send a message from a chair-lift going up a snowy slope. Of course you want to send an e-mail on a ski slope! And if you have to wait in the lift line, you can always play racquetball on your cell phone.

Probably your friend thought he was equipping his sixteen-year-old with a safety device when he conscientiously gave her a cell phone and urged her to call him from her car—until he got the first month's bill for 638 minutes, or until he assessed the fender bender that she showed him right in the middle of a board meeting using her camera phone. No emergency, you understand. This was after her Pretty Ricky's "Grind with Me" ring tone pro-vided just the excuse his board was waiting for to abandon him and his old-fashioned PowerPoint presentation. Talk about an occupational hazard!

Another aspect of the conspiracy against meaningful commu-nication in our contemporary lifestyle is talking on the phone while driving. "Celling" while driving is an especially salient example of superficial communication because it is competing with other demands on our senses. Although Martin Cooper cre-ated the car phone, as it was originally called, more than thirty years ago, most of us have retained a vestige of discomfort with it. C'mon, admit it. Our children and grandchildren thrive on it because it's the zeitgeist they were born into. Have you driven with a teen lately?

The automobile is no longer simply a vehicle for getting from one place to another—and the car manufacturers know it. Automobile technology's bells and whistles—stereo CD player, steering-wheel AM-FM access, global positioning system, drink holders—along with the cell or i-phone, that vital appendage of the twenty-first-century body, have turned the car into a mobile fast-food joint, entertainment venue, and communication center.

Our teen doesn't have to concentrate on getting to his destination because the GPS does it for him. What kind of mental-emotional engagement can be accomplished on a cell phone while one is eating, drinking, listening to hard rock, and driving? There are just so many brain synapses to go around. Indeed, a Harvard study says that up to three thousand deaths and three hundred thousand injuries a year are attributable to people talking on the phone while driving. Hands-free or hands-on, it's brain overload.

You bought into this aspect of contemporary lifestyle because of the hour-long commute you were forced to endure getting to and from work. After all, why shouldn't you use this semidowntime to eat breakfast, drink your morning coffee, get caught up with what happened in Asia while you were asleep, review your day's schedule, and confirm your appointments? Why shouldn't you use the sixty-two hours you were spending annually in traffic jams to respond to e-mail that came in after midnight? You reserved the commute home to make the daily call to your mother, who resides in an assisted-living apartment. She became used to the same perfunctory call each day. Her appreciation for your checking on her overrode her desire to converse about anything meaningful. She knew how busy you were.

"I've never been able to screw the right way!" my sister exclaims after I tell her that I'm concerned about our eighty-five-year-old mother living alone.

"What are you doing?" I ask.

"I'm changing a lightbulb. What did you think I was doing?"

"I thought you were talking to me," I say.

"Oh, darn! I dropped it!"

"Dropped what?" I ask.

"The bulb. Darn. Now I have to sweep it up!"

That's the way phone conversations go with my sister, who invariably is also doing her laundry or cleaning her horse stalls or finishing her grocery shopping or changing a lightbulb. If Freud were consulted, he would say, "Well, take your choice. She associates you with her dirty laundry or with her horses' tushes or with now-forbidden chips and dip or with illuminating her life."

Even those of us who are acutely aware of the intrusive rudeness of cell phones and the ambient cacophony created by their ring tones admit to their advantages when conversations go "over the top." You can always say, "You're breaking up. I can't hear you. Can you hear me? I've lost you." Too bad you didn't have a cell phone when you were a teenager—when breaking up was hard to do.

It's no wonder boomers invented e-mail. It's quicker than the U.S. Postal Service and more reliable than leaving recorded phone messages. At least you can *write* what you want to say and be done with it, and you can send a message to multiple receivers without the hassle of empathetic feedback. That's because e-mail doesn't require listening or empathetic response, 60 percent of which is facial and body language. Besides, there's something about the written word sent electronically through cyberspace that inhibits the expression of one's feelings, at least for your generation's way of thinking. And, of course, you learned from the trial of the World Trade Center saboteur Zacarias Moussaoui how retentive the memory on a hard drive can be.

But that's the point: e-mail and real-time instant messaging are yet further examples of communication technology that has conditioned us away from heart-to-heart communication and, certainly, empathetic listening. But don't try to tell that to your Gen-X children, who point, click, date, and cultivate (intimate?) relationships through chat rooms and e-dating sites. Indeed, your son's best friend "met" his Belgian fiancée in cyberspace. How can you fall in love with someone you've only *virtually* met? How do you develop rapport keyboard to keyboard? Maybe this is possible for echo boomers, who were nurtured by boomer parents who had forgotten how to listen. But wait! Since when do boomers operate under the radar? Cyber-romance is a growing trend for single boomers now, too. There's no dust on us!

Those of us who rely on e-mail are finding its efficacy diluted by overuse and cyberabuse. When I returned from a two-week vacation, I discovered over two hundred messages awaiting my mouse (including Nigerian get-rich-quick scams and several of the four million porn sites that rename themselves daily). "Enough already!" I screamed. "I'll get two e-mail addresses, one for commerce and one for friends. Never the twain shall meet."

Wrong. I have friends who must devote half their lives to forwarding everything from Adam and Eve jokes to the latest applications of antimatter. *And*, they forward these messages to everyone in their address books. The recipients, feeling compelled to respond with equivalent jokes or equally esoteric tidbits to everyone in their address books, open cc and add the addresses of everyone who received the original message. If one of these messages claims to have found the perfect Web site for ridding my yard of voles, my mouse just can't resist clicking on the *www* or the paperclip. Then somehow in the abracadabra of cyberspace, my inbox fills with "Dear Homeowner, You have been preapproved for $400,000 . . . Your credit is in no way a factor" and other scams labeling their subjects as "Re: Scoupage O'Desipamine HCl Miscell" when they're trying to sell me drugs. And there I am, again, in the quagmire of e-communication. Jupiter Research says that the typical home e-mail user receives over five thousand pieces of commercial e-mail yearly, 60 percent of which is spam and trash. What's more, these cyberspace bandits frequently make the audacious claim, "Your privacy is our concern." Oh, really.

Leery of these leeches who lurk on the Internet, we invest in the latest antispam and antivirus programs, which eat up memory and bog down speed, thereby discouraging our use of this communication technology. Moreover, my sending an e-mail doesn't mean the recipient will read it, because she, too, is getting mostly spam and trash. And if she does read my message, who knows how many others she may forward it to. Unless we're willing to share our thoughts with cyberspace or bequeath them to our hard drive, we don't e-mail. It's definitely not a means for soul-to-soul communication. And how did that #!@*%! computer know that I had a milestone birthday?

Have you attended a symphony concert lately? Even Borodin and Tchaikovsky need attention-grabbing backdrop visuals behind the orchestra performing their music. The twenty-first-century demand for multimedia entertainment is rooted, obviously, in what sells—that is, what appeals to an audience accustomed to multiple demands on the senses. That's us boomers, and certainly our echo-boomer children. And what about rock concerts? We may turn up our noses at the idea that the more visually shocking and deafeningly loud a concert is, the greater the appeal, but our generation set the precedent at Woodstock. Yes, yes, don't deny it. It was full-body (and spirit) immersion. The more senses the performance can engage, the greater the success. We created it and now we can't get away from it: deafening Dolby in movie theaters, and restaurant acoustics deliberately designed to subvert intimacy. In airports, grocery stores, and doctors' offices, on interminable telephone holds, and even in bookstores, we have grown so accustomed to background din (aka ambient music) that we have conditioned ourselves to tune it out. This reaction to unsolicited stimuli on our eardrums and consequent demands on our brains has become a reflex. We have taught ourselves how *not* to listen. It's become a survival skill in our world of the boom box, which was so named because of its reverberating speakers, not because our generation invented it.

Portentous of today's short-lived marriages—the shortest of which involve the entertainment industry's purveyors of contemporary music—is their beginning at wedding receptions where the band's decibels drown out conversation. Hence, the bride and groom, starting their marriage with acoustic trauma to their tympana, can't hear well enough to engage in meaningful conversation. What is the tacit message? That's the point: it's tacit. The vows might as well include, "And will you never presume to communicate with one another without including distracting or intruding sensory demands?"

But w-a-a-a-it a minute. Wasn't it the 1960s boomers who exclaimed, "You make me wanna (shout!)" as if shouting "a little bit louder" would help convey the meaning? What meaning? Indeed, popular rock had no problem substituting meaningless sounds for the sake of rhythm and rhyme. Expressions of the id might be an explanation, but any way you hear it, these nonsense sounds communicated nothing: "kookookashu, Mrs. Robinson"; "a wop bop alu la bop a wop bam boom"; "hey, hey, hey, hey, hey, hey, hey, hey"; "scoobie-dooba"; "hey, yea, yea, yea"; " ba-da, ba-da, da-da, ba-da, ba-da, da-da." Simon and Garfunkel sang the warnings in the "Sound of Silence." For a lot of reasons, boomers felt they weren't being heard in the sixties, and LPs and car radios conveyed our growing communication ineptness: we were "hearing without listening" and "talking without speaking." Like the Midnight Cowboy, we came to accept as a norm that everybody was talking at us but we didn't hear a word they were saying.

So, you say, what's the problem? Today's global businesses would collapse without e-mail, cell phones, pagers, and instant messaging. Cell phones alerted the heroic passengers of United Airlines Flight 93 and were used by search-and-rescue personnel to save countless lives after the 9/11 attacks. Satellite cable television gives us real-time updates on how we can help during tsunami, earthquake, and monster hurricane scourges. E-mail is such an expedient way to send holiday greetings to everyone in our address books, and who wants to attend a boring concert of *just* musical entertainment anymore?

The problem is that the development of late-twentieth-century technology has conditioned us to expect multiple sensory experiences from rapidly delivered communication, which undermines communication that is not exigent or entertaining. As a result, personal communication skills have deteriorated, and this has carried over to our relationships. Communication technologies, like all technologies, are tools. They are invented and implemented because they are supposed to facilitate communication in our fast-paced, distance-is-irrelevant world. We can't stuff the genie back into the lamp, nor would we want to. So, we'll deal with it. Superwoman will!

## CHALLENGE
### He Thinks Rapport Is Conversation with His Dog

This communication environment, along with the fact that men generally are weaker in the interpersonal and intrapersonal intelligences than women, makes communication the major problem in retirement marriages. The most significant marital role of retired Superwoman is taking leadership in empathetic communication. This is an imperative for several reasons: you personally need communication more than your male mate does; in retirement you've lost the daily collegial contact that, in part, fulfilled your need; you may have an innate talent for it; and the vitality of your marriage absolutely depends on it.

Women like to talk. That's what your husband says about your telephone conversations with your girlfriends. He says this only because your need is inscrutable to him. Women share their feelings with one another. In fact, they derive emotional security from confidantes. The depth of their friendships with other women is directly related to how much of themselves they feel comfortable revealing. Men do not need to talk in the same sense. Unlike women, they avoid the subjective in their conversations. Their talk is objective—about things, events, and processes. Rarely do they engage one another in conversations about their feelings or emotional needs. This is the reason why man's best friend is his dog, and woman's best friend is another woman. Unlike you, your husband's perception of the telephone is that it is a tool for expediting the necessary or the obligatory. Take, for example, the routine call he makes every Sunday at 10 a.m. to his brother, the manager of a golf course two states away. Here's the part you hear:

"Hello, Buck. Just thought I'd give you a call. How's the weather up there?"

"It's nice here, too. Did you have a lot of play on the course yesterday?"

"Is that right? Do you expect as many today?"

"That's good. Stock market took a hit last week."

"Yes, I know, the long run. Well, just thought I'd give you a call. Good to talk with you."

"Bye."

It's the same dialogue every week! Such shallow communication is sad to women. Really sad. Men miss so much of life by avoiding intimacy. Is it deliberate? Is it their nature or were they just raised that way?

John Gray says it's the way people are wired (men might as well be from Mars, and women from Venus). Leslie Brody and Judith Hall say the pattern is set early because girls develop language facility earlier than boys. Robert and Beverly Cairns trace men's and women's differing expectations of conversation to childhood ways of handling confrontation (boys with physical aggression, and girls with covert, verbal aggression). Daniel Goleman attributes to nature *and* nurture this "emotional gender gap" manifest in communication.

Even early in our college years, we formative superwomen knew we were suspending our disbelief as we watched Henry Higgins transform Eliza Dolittle into a woman befitting his social station. But we bought into this magical, romantic, happily-ever-after story nevertheless. Wouldn't it be loverly if we could magically transform our husbands into the sensitive, responsive men we desire? Dream on.

Retired superwomen are also up against an iconic machismo created by the social conditioning of their boomer husbands. Their fathers were the sons of Victorian Age fathers who distanced themselves from their children, whom they thought of and treated as mini-adults. Boomers' fathers were the brave and conquering heroes of World War II and the Korean conflict. Hardly warm and sensitive, they raised their sons to have a "stiff upper lip." Emotions were for women—or girlie men. For boomer Vietnam soldiers and (tragically) veterans, emotional detachment became a survival skill. Frank Sinatra's 1969 song "I Did It My Way" expresses the way most boomer men are expected to handle their emotions. Instead of stoically facing it all, standing tall, eating up and spitting out self-doubt, women talk it over with their girlfriends.

Biology, history, and culture all contribute to the problem at hand: boomer husbands' inability to communicate with heart. At least that's something you, as Superwoman, can change for your generation and—if your husband learns his lines well—for the next generation. He will become the model for those who follow and will pass along what he learns. Here's a strategy—for here and now—that you can use.

## STRATEGY

### Earn an A in Communication (Superwoman as Change Agent)

At this point in your life, the reasons for women having greater interpersonal skills—and empathetic communication is very definitely an interpersonal skill—don't really matter. You can't rewire the amygdala-cortical pathway in your husband's brain, nor can you undo his macho formative years on the playground and football field, much less the multisensory communication zeitgeist your generation created. What you can do, though, is teach him how to develop his half of sharing feelings. Otherwise, you will grow apart, and your relationship will become as mechanical and superficial as your required conversations.

Relationship books sell because they are about communication skills. Because a skill is a *learned* ability to do something competently, we read the books to learn to become better communicators and thereby foster desired relationships. If communication skills can be learned, then measurable objectives and a strategy for achieving them can be laid out. The problem is that *women* read relationship books, not men. Men don't like to read about their deficiencies—unless they can take a pill for them. That's another reason this communication thing is Superwoman's challenge.

Positive communication falls into four categories: acknowledgment, affirmation, appreciation, and affection. Depending on your husband's level of intimacy with everyone in his life, and especially with his wife, family, and friends, he should strive to communicate one or more of these four *A*'s. But knowing how to choose the correct *A* and its appropriate verbal (or nonverbal) initiation or response is part of the learning curve.

Although relationship experts may differ on the origins of the communication disparity between men and women, they agree that women must take the lead in teaching men the skills of emotional communication because women are more empathetic than men. Keep in mind, though, that of our eight forms of intelligence, the intrapersonal (self-understanding) and interpersonal (compassion and social responsibility) intelligences grow with age. These smarts aren't acquired with college degrees. They are developed during on-the-job-of-life experiences. Granted, women in general and the exceptional sensitive male may be more endowed with empathetic skills. But regardless of endowment, the longer one lives, the greater becomes one's ability in these areas. What does that mean for your seemingly insensitive husband? It means that he is more attuned to his own and others' feelings than he was when you married him, but he hasn't learned to communicate these feelings. It means he's trainable. These skills are easily learned if your husband always strives for an *A,* that is, strives to provide responses that express acknowledgment, affirmation, appreciation, or affection.

So now what? Just dig in and tell him what an insensitive lout he is and he'd better become more like you or else? You may be better suited for the facilitator role than he is, but even you may not have all the skills yet to start building the empathetic relationship your marriage needs. Chances are your husband is not even aware that he's not fulfilling your need for emotional intimacy, especially if you have quietly accommodated his deficiency all these years because you were so busy being Superwoman.

For someone to change, he must first recognize the need to change. Therefore, if you want him to be receptive to learning empathetic communication skills, you must convey to him the importance of communication in your relationship and in every relationship he deems valuable. You may never be able to get him to grasp as you do how crucial communication is in sustaining happiness, but his love for you should make him open to change.

Rent the movie *About Schmidt*. Schmidt's epiphany tells us it's never too late to start becoming a sensitive communicator. And if you do wait until it's too late, the results can be tragic.

Now that your husband agrees there may be a need to change, how do you go about teaching him empathetic communication skills? In the world of education, which is historically highly resistant to change, a methodology called the *rational problem-solving method* has been successfully applied to accomplishing change. It begins with an initial disturbance, or stimulus for change. From there the response activity is divided into six sequential steps:

1. define the problem or need;
2. decide to do something about it, that is, to make a change;
3. search for solutions;
4. choose the potential solutions;
5. apply one or more potential solutions; and
6. evaluate how well the solution(s) fixed the problem or satisfied the need.

This process repeats itself in a circular pattern until the original problem is solved. Then the same process is applied to new problems or needs as they arise.

Essential to this method is the change agent, the person who facilitates the process. The change agent as *catalyst* broaches the idea of a perceived need or problem; as *diagnostician* helps define the problem; as *resource linker* investigates and suggests potential solutions; as *implementer* helps put a change into practice; and as *evaluator* helps examine how well the solution fits the problem. For the functions of catalyst, diagnostician, implementer, and evaluator, the change agent must have communication and inter-personal-relations skills in order to accurately and unambiguously help define the problem and secure the trust of the partner to move toward change. For the function of resource linker, the change agent must have the information-accessing skills requisite for locating and isolating potential solutions. It's also suggested that the change agent have intimate knowledge of the behavior needing change. Based on these criteria, Superwoman is the logical choice for change agent. And because it is *your* need for empathetic communication that is not being met, you are the one who can define the problem(s) and evaluate the solution(s).

Before assuming the role of change agent, Superwoman needs to be armed with three cautionary details. First, don't underestimate the innate human resistance to change. Habit is comfortable; people feel threatened by change because of their fear of failure or their defensiveness in having one of their habits challenged. You can avert this resistance by preparing your husband for involvement in the change process. You have the advantage of knowing how adaptable your husband is to change, and you can help him understand the benefits of change and the rewards of new behavior.

Second, you absolutely must make this a team-of-two challenge. Your husband must perceive this change toward empathetic communication skills as something the two of you are working on together—not as something that's being forced upon him.

The third caveat is to recognize that you are not setting out to accomplish change for change's sake. Your role as change agent in this strategy is not to initiate change as an end in itself, but rather as the means to an end product. The change is the process, not the product. The end product, in this case, is communication behaviors perceived as new or different *and* satisfactory. Specifically, your and your husband's communication behaviors will be satisfactory when you are both able to respond at the appropriate time with the appropriate *A* of positive communication: acknowledgment, affirmation, appreciation, or affection. For the sake of a healthy marriage and the nearest you'll come to retirement bliss, you must convince hubby of this end product's importance to you—and to him. If you can teach him the empathetic communication skills that are applicable in your relationship, he will use these skills to enrich his relationships with family and friends. It is your responsibility as change agent to move him to the point where he is willing to change.

The change process begins with the perception of a specific communication problem that is thwarting your meaningful relationship. This becomes a stimulus for change in your husband's communication behavior. The six-step response sequence (page 64) is then started by your defining the way his behavior makes you feel (step 1). From your explanation of how his communication behavior makes you feel, your spouse can recognize his behavior as a good candidate for change. This is probably the hardest part: overcoming the psychological inertia, so to speak. You want to avoid sounding critical of him as a person. Such an approach is not constructive; it's destructive. You don't want to attack him. Instead, use your interpersonal intelligence to convey to him how his *specific behavior* makes you feel. What he did or said or didn't do or didn't say must be changed if you both are to develop a rapport that at least acknowledges one another's feelings.

Once your husband understands the effect of his behavior, he can decide to take action. This decision to change (step 2) has to be his; you, as change agent, cannot decide for him. Now, together, you can search for solutions (step 3). Potential solutions are described in myriad relationship guides you could look at together; you could offer some solutions you have already gleaned from reading the literature; or you as a couple could seek professional counseling. If your husband envisions this counseling taking place on a couch—the two of you together, lying horizontally—tell him that in intimacies, *c,* as in *communication,* comes before *s.* To jar him from this vision, just mention the hourly fee for professional counseling. That'll show him how serious you are!

From the sundry potential solutions you discuss together, the two of you choose one that is mutually acceptable (step 4) and apply it (step 5) through role-playing, thus developing—with practice—a new behavior in place of the initial behavior defined as the problem. The evaluation (step 6) will be how this new behavior makes you both feel. If this new behavior satisfies your need for one of the four *A*'s, then the change process has accomplished its objective.

The ultimate success of the solution, however, lies in how well it works over time. When your husband practices new, sensitive, and empathetic behavior, be sure to reinforce it with a smile, a kiss, a compliment on his behavior, or—why not—sex. After all, real communication—attending and responding to one another's feelings—is the most important part of intimacy. Real communication is a greater indication of his love for you than sex, and from the woman's point of view, real communication is a prerequisite for a fulfilling sexual relationship—or any intimacy between spouses.

The four *A*'s of empathetic communication are revealed in the following four scenarios that illustrate the gamut of husband-wife communication problems. In the first scenario, the wife seeks *acknowledgment* of feelings but gets a curt, dismissive response. In the second, she seeks *affirmation* of a request but gets no response. In the third, she seeks *appreciation* but gets an autobiographical response. And in the fourth, she seeks *affection* but gets destructive, hostile responses.

### Scenario
*Seeking Acknowledgment of Feelings*

You say, "I just can't help it. It's been five years since my father's death and I still can't control my sadness and feelings of guilt that I could have been more supportive of him after my parents' divorce. It seems that every February I feel depressed and want to cry all the time."

Your husband replies, "You'll get over it. You always have. What do you think we should have for dinner?"

If you retreat without verbalizing how this sort of response makes you feel, you will be reinforcing this kind of insensitivity to all future expressions of your feelings. The important element to remember is that you as change agent must define the problem about his behavior that needs changing. You might say the following:

"Honey, if you will listen to me empathetically, you will be helping me deal with my feelings. I need to have you acknowledge the legitimacy of my feelings. You are the only person in whom I can confide my vulnerability about this. When you dismiss my feelings, I feel you don't care about the one thing in my life that evokes the most pain. I feel as if you don't care about me. I need to share my feelings with you. Please listen to how I feel."

With this kind of response you have stated the problem: he is not acknowledging the communication of your feelings. If, however, you were to respond, "You never care about anything that really matters to me; this is the same sort of callous response that I always get from you," you would be defeating your purpose. You would not be articulating the problem behavior; you would be criticizing your husband. Remember, this is a *rational* problem-solving method. Be rational *and* communicate your feelings. This is a big challenge for your interpersonal skills, but you can do it. Especially if you keep in mind what's at stake.

From your impassioned and rational statement of the problem, your husband should understand the need to change his behavior. He could ask you, for example, "Well, what do you want me to do?"

You might respond, "You could acknowledge my feelings. I loved my father. I also love my mother. But I felt divided loyalties after my parents' divorce. I feel my mother successfully pulled me away from my father and I feel guilty about neglecting my dad."

He now says, "I understand how you feel. But you did the best you could at the time. I think your father knew that. He certainly knew how much you loved him."

### Scenario
#### Seeking Affirmation of a Request

You say, "Honey, I'm going outside to transplant a couple of hydrangeas. If Jeff from Boxwoods calls back, could you please call me to the phone or . . ." Before you can finish, he walks out of the room. Assuming he's listening, though, you complete your request: ". . . or bring me the portable if you leave? This call is important to me."

His apparent choice not to affirm your request communicates to you that he doesn't consider your request worthy of his response; nevertheless, you assume he heard you. So you don your mud shoes and cowhide gloves and commit yourself to nature. When you return to the house a couple hours later, you discover that he has left. No note. You check the message machine and, sure enough, Jeff called an hour ago. You're upset because now you'll have to play phone tag. Actually, you're furious, but not because of the impending phone tag.

When your husband returns, you ask him angrily, "Why didn't you bring me the portable phone when you left?"

He replies, "I didn't know you were expecting a call. I had to run to Radio Shack to get DSL filters."

As change agent in this situation, you must keep your cool and rationally state the problem: "It makes me feel insignificant when you don't listen to me and ignore my requests."

Your husband responds, "I wasn't ignoring you. I had my mind on our Earthlink connection problem. After you went outside I got a call from tech support and had to go get these DSL filters to see if they will solve the problem."

Aha. It wasn't that he *chose* not to listen; his brain wiring *prevented* him from hearing you because he had his mind on something else—his *own* need. In your search for solutions, you consult Michael Gurian's *What Could He Be Thinking? How a Man's Mind Really Works.*

Compared to women, you learn, men have 25 percent less corpus callosum, the bundle of nerves that connects the brain's right and left hemispheres. Because feelings and thoughts are experienced in the right brain but are communicated in the left brain, the male is at a marital disadvantage because of his dearth of corpus callosum. (Somehow, you remember, he always seemed to make the connection disarmingly foolproof in courtship.) In addition, the male brain's larger amygdala, which has less of a link to other parts of the emotional-control brain, explains why men choose a physically aggressive response to a situation instead of responding with tender feelings or conversation (think Stanley in *A Streetcar Named Desire* or Bruce Willis in the *Die Hard* movies). Furthermore, men produce less oxytocin, a neurotransmitter linked to cuddling and caretaking.

Obviously, here we need a redefinition of the communication problem. His walking away from you as you were attempting to communicate is not a conscious act of ignoring you. Nor is he deliberately not listening to your request. Nevertheless, your need to communicate is not being met. Given his brain biology, your husband may not be able to learn a new behavior that will prevent recurring instances of this problem.

But you, as Superwoman, can! Kryptonite? Nope. How about a little of that female sensitivity you're always boasting about?

Remember that communication is a mutual concern in the husband-wife partnership. Living with this man 24/7 now, it would be insensitive of you to assume that he will process your request if you blurt it from the next room or when he is enthralled in his sixth Grisham novel. In a kind and respectful manner, you will have to secure his attention. You don't know what he's thinking about, but if you want to convey a request, you have to make sure that he has shifted his attention to what you're saying. Face him, look him in the eye, take his hand or put your arm on his shoulder, and ask, "What's going on in that handsome head?" or "Hi! You sure look cute today. What's up?" Maybe a little swagger of the hips would jar him. After it is clear that he has shifted his attention to what you are saying, you can relay your request. It may sound silly in a thirty-plus-year relationship, but a sincere thank-you or a spontaneous kiss will reinforce the importance of his affirming your communicated need.

A cautionary sidebar: Because of your husband's dearth of corpus callosum, be forewarned about getting inaccurate telephone messages through him. For example, your husband tells you that Brenda said the cat food is beside the sliding door, and you resort to feeding your vacationing neighbor's kitty albacore tuna because you can't find her food. Later you learn from Brenda that she had said the cat food was on top of the chimney shelf. Now she has a spoiled cat, and you have a friend doubting your reliability. Another example is when your husband says that Joan asked you to add water to her pool if the level falls below the skimmers. Because it rained every day she was gone, you knew the water level was OK. Later you learn that she had asked that you empty her skimmers of clogging mimosa blossoms in case it rained. Oh, well, no more free swims next door.

And then there's the message from your husband that Janie called, but she will call back later. Your offended friend calls you a week later wanting to know why you didn't call her back when you got in. No telling what your husband was doing when the telephone rang, but obviously he was not able to switch gears. Could this be another reason men hate the telephone? Could it be that they view it as an interruption, an intrusion on their concentration? But be patient with his lack of corpus callosum, and be sure he has shifted his attention before you indict his insensitivity—which, as this scenario has illustrated, may be a pejorative for inadequate male brain wiring.

### *Scenario*

*Seeking Appreciation*

You say, "I have a problem getting my mother to appreciate anything I've accomplished on my own. You know that newspaper article about my volunteer work with the Council for International Visitors? Mom's only comment was, 'Why do you want to encourage all those foreigners to come here?' And then, about my garden—my splendid perennial garden—her comment is, 'You'll learn. It's much smarter to let your yard go wild. Too much upkeep, but you'll learn.' You'd think she could at least say something complimentary about my daylilies."

Your husband, who has listened to you autobiographically but not empathetically, says, "Yes, I know what you mean. My uncle, to the day he died, thought I should have stayed with the Navy. He discouraged me from going to law school and he never *once* acknowledged my success as a lawyer. I just ignored my uncle. You need to do the same thing. Just ignore your mother's judgments on your life."

You state the problem: "I understand your uncle's influence on your life, but you overcame it. Good for you! But I haven't come to terms with my mother's judgment of my life. I'm trying to help her deal with her aging, and she seems to criticize me and my life more and more. I need to have you understand me, how I feel, what causes me pain. I ask you to listen to what I say with your heart, and not as a cue for telling me your parallel experiences. I can't ignore how my mother makes me feel. She really doesn't appreciate anything I've accomplished, and from your response I don't think you understand my need for appreciation either."

Now your husband realizes that he has left you unfulfilled and that you genuinely need to have him listen to you empathetically. He is willing to change his response. But how? Remember that he may lack the intuitive ability to know how to listen empathetically. That's where you, as change agent, and the experts come in. Consult the experts! Guide your spouse to them. As much as you'd like to think otherwise, your communication problems with your retired spouse are not unique. They're *generic*. And you're educated. Right? Rational in your problem solving? Adaptable to change? You darn well better be, or else twenty-first-century history will footnote you instead of putting you in chapter titles. Be all the Superwoman you can be!

Start with Stephen Covey's fifth habit in *The Seven Habits of Highly Effective People*. He instructs his readers to listen with the "intent to understand . . . emotionally as well as intellectually." What thwarts such listening, he says, is the autobiographical response grown out of the "intent to reply, to control, to manipulate." Although we may not be conscious of it, such listening is selfish because it interprets all that is said in terms of one's own experience. Covey defines four varieties of autobiographical responses: "We *evaluate*—we either agree or disagree; we *probe*—we ask questions from our own frame of reference; we *advise*—we give counsel based on our own experience; or we *interpret*—we try to figure people out, to explain their motives, their behavior, based on our own motives and behavior."

As an antidote to listening autobiographically, Covey offers four developmental stages to empathetic listening: mimicking content, rephrasing content, reflecting feeling, and rephrasing the content and reflecting the feeling. The fourth stage is what you're aiming for, but you, as change agent, will probably have to help your husband get there incrementally—at least until he masters the skill.

By *mimicking content,* your husband is training himself simply to listen to what you say: "You have a problem getting your mother to acknowledge anything you've accomplished on your own. She thinks you're encouraging foreigners with your work on the council, and she thinks you should let your perennial garden go wild because it's too much maintenance."

By *rephrasing content,* your husband is putting into his own words what you said. He is thinking about what you said with his left brain—the reasoning, logical side: "It's a problem to you that your mother doesn't recognize what you've achieved. She says you're helping foreigners with your work on the council, and she thinks that eventually you'll learn that your perennial garden is too much trouble."

The third stage, *reflecting feeling,* forces your husband's right brain into operation. Here he is gleaning your feelings from what you said: "You feel unappreciated. You feel indicted, hurt, and disappointed."

Now that he is attending to the way you feel about what you are saying as well as to what you are saying, he is ready to combine the second and third stages into the fourth, *rephrasing the content and reflecting feeling:* "You feel your mother doesn't appreciate your accomplishments. You are proud of your contributions to the international community through the council, but your mother criticizes your public recognition because of her prejudice against foreigners. You are hurt and disappointed that your mother won't acknowledge the beauty of your perennial garden, the hobby that expresses your soul and from which you derive so much joy. And you want me, because you know you can't communicate with your mother, to appreciate your feelings about your relationship with her."

As your husband learns to rephrase the content and reflect the feeling in what you communicate to him, he will be employing the first three A's of communication: acknowledgment of what you say, affirmation of the importance of what you say, and appreciation for the feelings you express. He is enabling you to deal with your problem with your mother just by empathetically listening to you. Wow! What a metamorphosis! What a tender, understanding, sensitive man he has become. After all these years, you feel emotionally drawn to him as never before. It's a new level of intimacy and mutual understanding that pervades every aspect of your marriage. As Barbra Streisand sings, "With one person, one very special person / A feeling deep in your soul / Says you were half, now you're whole."

At last your husband has learned to respond in a way that reflects his understanding of what you want to communicate to him. He has thus made himself a worthy source of advice in your eyes. You now feel comfortable asking him, "What do you think about my problem with my mother? Is it my fault or hers? What should I do?"

Perceiving himself as trusted and needed, he can make some logical and sensitive suggestions: "Maybe you shouldn't seek your mother's appreciation for your accomplishments when she can't relate to them. She didn't have your education or your opportunities for professional accomplishment. Your mother criticizes your work with international visitors because of her prejudice against anyone who was not born an American citizen. I don't think she means to be cruel about your garden. Remember, she had a beautiful rose garden herself thirty years ago. Maybe your garden reminds her of what old age has made her give up. And maybe your accomplishments remind her of what her generation couldn't provide to women and what the Depression deprived her of."

Or your husband might say, "Sounds to me like your mom could use you as a communication change agent. Why don't you transform her into an empathetic listener and teach her how to let go of her autobiography and strive for the four *A*'s of empathetic communication? Or, better yet, why don't you let me teach her? I could tell her I've learned this wonderful technique and have become the sensitive husband that her adoring daughter has always wanted me to be. Besides, it sure would help her develop a more nurturing relationship with our Gen-X children, not to mention her great-grandchildren. Sounds like she could use some diversity training, too. Think your mother would listen to *me?*"

Doubtful . . .

### Scenario
#### Seeking Affection

Let this final example serve as a solemn warning: if you don't take the initiative to cultivate positive, mutually nurturing communication skills, your relationship could become the kind of destructive competition Martha and George perpetuate in Edward Albee's *Who's Afraid of Virginia Woolf?* If you're not familiar with the play or if you've forgotten a lot of it, rent the film and watch it with your husband. Richard Burton plays George; Elizabeth Taylor is Martha. From the scuttlebutt about their real-life marriage, you don't have to suspend much disbelief. Despite their desire for affection from one another, these characters portray what a marriage can become when partners don't empathetically communicate. Martha and George's relationship is built on pernicious manipulation, sadistic degradation, innuendo, double entendre, humiliation, insult, and caustic rejoinders. Because Martha cruelly dwells on George's weaknesses, his responses are defensive; her responses are offensive.

You don't want a relationship built on caustic repartee; you want one built on respect, kindness, mutual understanding, affection—in other words, rapport. The destruction caused by words is powerful and sometimes irredeemable. Surely you remember from freshman psychology that how we see ourselves is largely determined by how we believe others see us.

As far as you know, you have only one lifetime to make your individual contribution to the progress of humanity. Start with the person with whom you *chose* to share this lifetime. Be kind. Be respectful. Be patient. Don't look at him as a glass half empty; look at him as a glass almost full and see yourself as the power to help him fill it—helping fulfill you both. Set the example for empathetic communication and help your husband learn the skills that can enrich his life, your life, and the lives of others he loves. Help him communicate this love. Sometimes all it takes is a warm touch, a smile, and—at least once daily—an "I love you."

A final word: Be glad you're Superwoman and your track record carries clout. Be so glad that you were born into this era of opportunity for women. Your husband knows that you're his partner—interested in his and, therefore, your collective welfare. Be grateful that you're *not* a desperate housewife, the cultural cure for which just a generation earlier was Nembutal, Seconal, and later Valium. Remember *Valley of the Dolls*? Did you know that in 1969 Americans ingested 2.3 billion "chill pills" annually? Perhaps Stanley in *A Streetcar Named Desire* and Martha in *Who's Afraid of Virginia Woolf?* needed antidepressants. They were clinical cases that could legitimately have used them. You've moved on.

## OBJECTIVE 4

# Put the Works in That "Sandwich"
### (What Parents and Kids Want)

Between 1990 and 2000 the number of Americans eighty-five years and older increased 38 percent. In this cohort are the parents of first-wave boomers. This demographic trend reflects what we already know: people are living longer. At the other end of the age spectrum, there's another trend: people are maturing later. Young people aren't assuming the responsibilities traditionally associated with adulthood—moving out of the nest, holding a job, getting married, having a family—until their late twenties. For most, college has become a five- or six-year program. Sociologists say Americans are now reaching adulthood at twenty-six years old.

What does this mean for the retiring baby-boom generation? As I noted earlier, it means that we're the meat in the intergenerational sandwich (which could be a club sandwich if you're grandparents!). What you're up against are—on the top—your parents, who won't admit they're old, or at least old enough for your intervention in their daily lives, and—on the bottom—your children, who refuse to grow up but won't admit their dependency on you. No problem for the boom generation that refuses to grow old! This age-expectation thing is all a bunch of nonsense. You'll give 'em both the works!

## CHALLENGE
### What Happened to Mom and Dad? I Thought They Existed to Validate Me

From the song my mother sang to me as early as I can remember, I remember this stanza especially:

*You're the cream in my coffee,*
*You're the salt in my stew.*
*You will always be my necessity*
*I'd be lost without you!*

This stanza meant to me what my parents validated through their words and deeds: they existed for me and for me only, except maybe also for my boomer siblings. Their lives, I thought, began with my birth. What preceded was of no consequence. I was their princess, their be-all and end-all. They lived for me and my future. The Great Depression and World War II had taught them that they should put all they had into an enduring investment: their child, me. So what if they made sacrifices to educate me and give me everything they never had? I'm worth it! I'm paying them off with my success. I am the validation of their lives, their existence. It's me, my challenges, and my children they center their lives on.

"Gary won his tennis match today!" you jubilantly report to your mom while you're driving home from the tournament.

She responds, "I think I forgot to put—oh, what's the name of that stuff?—on Morris, because we have fleas all over the house," or "Your father slipped in the shower this morning, and I had to call 9-1-1 to help him up."

Here it is, one of the great epiphanies in a boomer's life: my parents no longer live to validate me; their focus has shifted to themselves. This is a major turning point in your relationship with your parents. You realize that it's now up to you to validate *their* changing view of life. And that song your mother sang to you? "You will always be my necessity / I'd be lost without you" has a whole new meaning.

Unless a catastrophic health event suddenly strikes, your parents will decline gradually. Whether the decline is mental or physical, it inexorably narrows their control over their lives. This is hard for us boomers to accept because we've convinced ourselves that we have control over a vitality that lasts forever. How could we have mortal parents? And it's very difficult for our parents, because they're the great generation—survivors of the Depression, World War II, the Cold War, and parenting kids who rocked around the clock and later were always on some side of a picket line.

Superwoman sees the cues: her parents' waning interest in her life and waning interest in the world beyond their immediate needs. Geriatric physiology and psychology tell us that life closes in on us in very old age. We cannot control the self-absorption. Why should your ninety-five-year-old mother-in-law care about your daughter's mountain-climbing expedition if she can't make it to the bathroom without assistance, or, worse, if she can't remember where the Tetons are? Understanding life on your parents' terms, seeing life from their perspective, requires sensitivity, Superwoman's sensitivity.

Thou shalt not, in the name of Superwoman, swoop down upon the home of thy parents—or worse, thy parents-in-law—and declare: "God said, 'Honor thy father and thy mother,' and my interpretation of this is that you'd better take orders from me from here on out. It's for your own good! Now get thee to a nursing home!"

No, no, no! It doesn't much matter what the declaration is or where it comes from; they're not going to buy it. They didn't buy into Hitler's declaration that he was going to take over the world, Khrushchev's declaration that he was going to bury them, or your declaration that they didn't have *any idea* how it felt to be *really* in love. These parents of ours are tough—as they eternally remind us: walking miles to school in the snow, sharing one car (is this possible?), living without air-conditioning (is that living?), cooking without microwaves *or* aluminum foil (how do you do that?).

What you want to achieve—with the empathy, respect, and love they deserve and have earned—is not their long-term care, but their long-term independence, independence that validates the dignity of their lives. What you want to avoid is the sudden realization that change is necessary *today* because planning was not done yesterday. Recent U.S. census figures show that centenarians are the fastest-growing segment of the population, their numbers doubling in the 1990s to seventy thousand. Statistically, even more of our parents will live to this age. Our retirement affords the time to plan for our parents' long-term independence.

But wait! Who is the operative "you" in accomplishing this objective in boomer retirement? Just because Superwoman has always been the one responsible for the Mother's and Father's Day cards, the birthday gifts, the holiday dinners, the grandbaby pictures, and the thoughtful phone calls and visits doesn't mean she has all the skills for helping parents plan for their future. In a marriage the husband and wife share their parents, sort of like *mi casa es su casa.* And in retirement you share responsibility for parents. So how does your husband come in on this caring you've always anchored?

Again, Superwoman initiates a strategic plan. You and your husband define the objective: *We will help our parents achieve long-term independence.* And you both agree on the core value behind this objective: *It is critical to make our parents feel in charge; they are entitled to as much autonomy as is safe.* Again, Superwoman takes the lead in devising a strategy to achieve this objective.

## STRATEGY
### Apply Customer-Service Skills

One of the effects of the global competition you experienced midway through your career was the new approach to customer service. You were retrained to deal with people outside and inside the organization without condescension or humiliation. You may have been the boss, but you weren't supposed to be perceived as controlling or demanding. The idea was to build trust and mutual respect and then work as a team toward a common goal. Why can't these skills you learned help your husband with parental care? As Superwoman you will reengineer your husband's relationship with both sets of parents by applying customer-service skills.

You both may still shake in your boots when these strong disciplinarians stubbornly bark, "I'm still your father (or mother)!" but your husband must realize that he is the stronger lion now. Your applied skills will respectfully, empathetically, and lovingly achieve your objective of putting the works in that intergenerational sandwich. Your husband will understand that you are willing to facilitate as lioness if he can walk the roar—while protecting his parents' pride. To this end, you and your husband will—

- maintain rapport with your parents;
- solve problems together with your parents;
- follow up and take action, if necessary;
- think of yourselves and your parents as a team;
- prepare and empower your parents while continuing to monitor progress.

To maintain rapport with parents, boomer couples first have to build the foundation for the rapport. To ensure your parents' long-term independence, there are some very basic, practical issues to address. These issues fall under the same questions you've always asked when assaying your life, particularly at passage points: *Where am I? Where do I want to go? How do I get there?* Your retirement is an opportune time for your parents to address these questions about their own lives because they realize, "Oh, my gosh, we're the *parents* of a retired child!" If they've been in denial about their age, your milestone should be their wake-up call—or eye-opener if they're hard of hearing.

In addition, your transition to your second adulthood may give your parents a feeling of a new common ground with you. As you think about where you are, where you want to go, and how you're going to get there, you could work as a team with your parents. (Ah, remember all that team-building training you endured in the 1980s? Maybe there's an application here.) With your parents you will tackle some basic issues that need to be nailed down before . . . before . . . you know, before you start associating nails with something else.

Physical independence and fiscal independence are central to your parents' long-term control over their future. Your customer-service skills, though, have taught you that these issues should be addressed in the context of relationship building, not as items on the day's agenda. In building trust and mutual respect, the first requirement is the all-important empathetic communication. So listen up, boomer husbands, you're on a winning team with Superwoman!

### Customer Service
#### Maintain Rapport

Remember the boomer epiphany about your parents? It is fore-shadowed in cues that reflect your parents' growing detachment from the everyday events in your life. Then there's the revelation that Mom and Dad no longer exist to validate you. The focus of their lives has shifted to themselves. Finally, you realize that those strong authority figures in your life are losing their strength—or authority.

Your husband, no doubt, doesn't—or can't—pick up on the subtle cues (Dad forgot my birthday; Mom broke her hip), but your greater endowment of intuition, sensitivity, corpus callo-sum—whatever—can alert your husband. Together you can build a new kind of conversation with your parents: one that focuses on them. Imagine that! If you're going to build rapport with an octo-genarian or a nonagenarian or certainly a centenarian, you have to see life through *their* eyes. They need to be assured that you understand *their* needs, uppermost of which is their need for independence.

Once this rapport is established, maintain it by opening con-versations with questions or comments—sincerely felt and expressed—about them: "Is your shoulder still hurting, Mom?" "I hope you had a good night's sleep last night." And seek their advice. Let them know that their opinions are valued, and they will value yours.

Tell your husband to call on the empathetic communication skills he learned from you. Remind him of how his striving to earn an *A* in communication has improved your marital relationship. Now, in conversations with his parents, he should also listen with heart and then respond with acknowledgment, affirmation, appre-ciation, or affection. The following conversational scenarios illus-trate how rapport can be built and maintained with your parents when these skills are applied.

### Acknowledging Your Mother-in-Law's Limitations

Your mother-in-law says, "I just don't have the energy I used to have. I would love to, but I just can't prepare dinner for the five of us anymore when you visit."

Your husband's insensitive reply: "OK, Mom, that's no prob-lem for us. We'll eat later."

Your husband's response that empathetically acknowledges your mother-in-law's limitations: "We understand, Mom. We'll bring dinner, or we'll prepare it when we get there so we can all enjoy dinner together. Or, if you and Dad feel like it, we could all go out to eat."

### Affirming Your Father-in-Law's Values

Your father-in-law says, "You know, the problem with you young folks is that you don't take time to eat a healthy meal, especially breakfast. You wolf down some health bar or swig some nutrient concoction without even sitting down, unless you're sitting behind the wheel on your way somewhere. Now me, I think the answer to a long and healthy life is three squares a day. That means a breakfast of two fried eggs, bacon or sausage—and not that low-fat turkey disguised as pork—grits with red-eye gravy, your mother's made-from-scratch pancakes with maple syrup, and her biscuits with *real* butter and jam. And three cups of coffee, the high-test kind with the reason for drinking it left in, with *real* cream and three teaspoons of *real* sugar. Now that's the way to start a day!"

Your husband's affirming response: "That sounds delicious, Dad. I think you and Mom should continue to enjoy breakfasts like that."

Your husband resists the temptation to lecture about cholesterol and sugar. His father is a robust eighty-six. His generation's values don't have to be yours. At his age, he is entitled to the dietary idiosyncrasies that evidently have sustained his good health. Go figure, NIH!

### Expressing Appreciation to Your Mother

At your birthday celebration with family and close friends, your mother says, "I can't believe my baby girl is celebrating her fifty-ninth birthday!"

Your appreciative response: "Mom, if it weren't for you I wouldn't have birthdays. The earliest I remember was my fifth birthday. You organized a party. You invited my whole kindergarten class. We played musical chairs and popped balloons. Then we ate chocolate cake that you had baked."

Your mother says, "I can't believe you remember that day. It was such a happy occasion for me."

"Mom, whenever I remember highlights from my childhood, you're always in the picture. I remember when you read Hans Christian Andersen's 'The Ugly Duckling' to me and when you made me walk around the house with a book on my head because I cried about being the tallest person in the second grade. I remember when you and Dad went along with my backyard funeral service for Kitty Whiskers. I remember when you bought me my first crinoline. And, Mom, every time I look at Grandma's silver service here in the dining room I think of you—and Grandma, of course. It represents my heritage of strong, intelligent women."

Superwoman and her husband resolve to seize opportunities like this to express appreciation to their parents. Expressing gratitude, moreover, is good for us. Psychologists tell us that cultivating a habit of gratitude (or an attitude of gratitude) is a cure for the Type D personality, characterized by irritability, faultfinding, impatience, and a short temper. It makes us better people when we show appreciation for what others have done for us. Few have done more for us than our parents.

### Verbalizing Affection to Your Mother-in-Law

Your mother-in-law says, "Well, I do what I can do, which isn't much more than reading or watching TV. But I do love you all."

Your hearts melt. It's rare that her post-Victorian upbringing allows her to express feelings. You and your family are all she has left, her living legacy. You more than love her. You admire her, you venerate her, you stand in awe of her. Well, then, say it! Show it!

And get your husband on the same page with you. You and your husband respond, "We love you, too, Mom. And we appreciate you for being so strong, for always being optimistic, and for showing us how to be responsible adults."

In striving for one of the four *A*'s of empathetic communication with your parents, you are establishing a relationship of mutual understanding and trust. As this rapport builds, you can look for opportunities to address the issues of your parents' long-term independence.

### Customer Service
#### Solve Problems Together
Your husband says, "I know it must have really scared you two when Dad slipped in the shower and couldn't get up. It's a good thing you were there, Mom, and called 9-1-1. Have you heard about home modifications called 'universal design features'?"

### Home Is Where the Heart Is and Where
### the Grab Bars Should Be

"Universal design features are modifications that improve access and use for people of all ages and physical abilities. The Remodelers Council of the National Association of Home Builders, the NAHB, estimates that one-quarter of the money we baby boomers spend on remodeling is devoted to what's called aging-in-place modifications. Grab bars in showers—the ones you see in hotels now—and higher toilets are becoming chic and smart. There are lots of other universal design elements that can make a home more user-friendly, such as easy-to-grab cabinet and door handles. Why don't we both call the NAHB and ask them about local remodelers who have had their certified aging-in-place training?"

Your mother-in-law responds, "That's interesting. I'll take care of it, Honey. Don't worry about us. We can take care of ourselves."

### Customer Service
*Follow Up and Take Action, If Necessary*
In several months, if Mom and Dad have not made arrangements to have grab bars installed in their shower . . .

### Become the Pro in Proactive

Your husband says, "I've located someone who installs grab bars. Here's his number. Would you like to call him to put one in your shower, or should I call him for you? Remember what you always say? A stitch in time saves 9-1-1 calls, and an ounce of prevention can be worth a pound of security."

### Customer Service

*Be a Team*
Your mother-in-law says, "I've been thinking about what you said about modifying our house with universal design features. And then I thought about our bedroom being upstairs. Those stairs are getting to be a challenge."

Your husband replies, "Well, Mom, you're really smart to be thinking ahead like this. Have you thought about your options? You could install an elevator or a lift on the stairwell, or you could add a bedroom or convert a room downstairs to a bedroom."

### The Best Things in Life May Be Free, but
### Long-Term Independence Isn't

His mom answers, "Yes, but I don't know if those changes would be worth their cost if we needed—you know—someone to help care for us. Your father seems to be getting forgetful, and I'm not able to look after him every minute. Besides, we can't take care of the yard anymore, and this house is really more space than we need. I'm not really sure what we can afford."

You say, "Bob and I are doing a little thinking about the future ourselves. Financial analysts say we adults need to assess our net worth and then update it annually. At any stage of life, our lifestyle should operate within the parameters of what we can afford. You've got to know what you've got in order to know where you're going. That's why the first chapter or two of financial planning books is always a discussion of net worth. Basically, it's an itemization of the value of your assets minus your liabilities. I know you and Dad did this a while ago, but have you updated it lately?"

Your mother-in-law answers, "No, not since Bob's dad retired. That's been, what? Twenty years ago?"

You respond, "Well, Mom, it's time you took the reins. And Bob and I will help you. In addition to considering routine and predictable expenses, which inflate at 3 percent a year, if you're thinking about making major changes to your house, assistance in caring for Dad, or moving, you have to know what your resources are.

"Bob and I discovered a really smart way to update our net worth. Since you have to revisit yours anyway, you could use the same framework we use. [*Refer to the chart on the next page.*] Alongside the description and value of each asset, we include its title, that is, who owns it (individual, tenants in common, joint tenants with rights of survivorship, or community property), and its designated primary and secondary beneficiaries. The actual designation of beneficiaries is done in a will or a trust, but it's helpful to make note of it here as well.

"This sort of chart is one way. Financial journalist Jane Bryant Quinn suggests another strategy. She advises using the categories of Quick Assets (parts of your net worth always on tap for emergencies), Restricted Assets (those attainable only by paying a penalty), and Slow Assets (ones that take a long time to sell or assets that you least want to liquidate). Quinn suggests that alongside the column for the amount of liabilities there should also be a column for interest rate.

## ESTIMATING NET WORTH

| | Value ($) | Title | Designated Beneficiary Primary/Secondary |
|---|---|---|---|
| *ASSETS* | | | |
| Real Estate | | | |
|   House | | | |
|   Land | | | |
|   Rental property | | | |
|   Vacation property | | | |
| Bank Accounts | | | |
|   Checking | | | |
|   Savings | | | |
| CDs | | | |
| Other Investments | | | |
| Other Major Assets | | | |

| | Value ($) | Person/Company |
|---|---|---|
| *LIABILITIES* | | |
| Mortgages | | |
| Home Equity Loans | | |
| Credit Card Debts | | |
| Other Major Liabilities | | |

"You can download forms for calculating net worth by entering 'net worth calculation' in a search engine like Google. Or you can make your own spreadsheet or just write it on a sheet or two of paper. I don't think you need an attorney or an accountant for this. I'll be happy to help you. I can help you structure a format you like, and then you can fill in the blanks if that's what you prefer doing. If this net worth is updated every year, it can also serve as a very good approximation of your net taxable estate.

"And since we're on the topic of taxable estate, Mom, you should know that the maximum federal estate tax rate for portions of estates over $2 million is (or was) 46 percent in 2006, and 45 percent in 2007 through 2009. In 2010 you can die and leave gazillions to your heirs and not pay a penny in *federal* estate tax. But who wants to die a millionaire as soon as 2010? This is where estate planning, especially for us boomers, becomes applicable. In 2011, if Congress doesn't decide otherwise, an estate will pay federal tax of 55 percent on a net worth over $1 million. That could be just an ouch or it could be a major laceration for a small, family-owned business."

### To Nest the Egg or Scramble It

If the planets are aligned, or rather if your parents have intelligently aligned their spheres of spending/saving/investing during their earning years, they'll have plenty of options for their future. Sadly, most boomers aren't doing that. Many people seem to think our consumer-driven economy means they are driven to consume; when they calculate their net worth they may find liabilities exceeding assets. The twenty-first century is teaching us we're building a retirement house of straw if we rely on just one company's stock (à la WorldCom or Enron) or on Social Security (the hot where-will-it-be-in-the-future topic). But that's a problem we boomers face along with our children and our children's children.

At least you can share your anxiety about retirement financial security with your parents. But your goal here is help your parents know where they are so they know which options are open to them. Regardless of their financial profile, monthly income needs to be interfaced with monthly expenses to see how money is flowing. Is it flowing upstream (in which case some of those quick assets may need to be tapped) or downstream (into a comfortably deepening reservoir of assets)?

Again, as boomers, you may ask how large this reservoir should be for your own future. There is no crystal ball to tell us that, but you can bet on one thing: we're going to live very long lives. We need to know if we're swimming with dolphins or sharks. If the latter, we need to change course.

Your parents may want to seek guidance from an estate planner, investment consultant, accountant, or estate attorney. But they absolutely must know where they are financially before they can decide where they can go. And at this stage in their lives, this means literally where they can go. Actuaries still give us boomers time to incubate our nest eggs or start laying new ones. Our parents don't have this luxury. It may be time for them to scramble, poach, or fry.

### It's the Ninth Inning—Help Your Parents Make a Home Run!

Your mother-in-law says, "Not only is your dad getting forgetful and the house more than we can manage, but we don't have the friends around here that we used to. When Howard died, Sally moved to Chicago to be near her children. Our other neighbors are all in their thirties and forties. Your dad and I miss people closer to our age whom we can talk to and do things with. And it sure would be nice if your dad could walk right out onto a putting green. We feel like fish out of water here now."

Your husband responds, "Maybe you should consider a new pad in a different pond. Now that you know what you can afford, I'll help you with the research. I do think you should keep Dad's growing memory loss in mind—in your mind, not his—and be realistic about your future. Even friends of *mine* are moving to retirement communities. Did you know that over eighteen million baby boomers will be turning sixty during the next five years? And the pace picks up after that because of all those babies born in the 1950s and early 1960s. Imagine how that's going to redefine the retired American lifestyle! By the middle of the century analysts predict there will be 834,000 centenarians. That's my generation! Wow! We're going to live a very long time. I think we ought to look into retired lifestyle options together!"

Your mother-in-law says, "That sounds like a good idea, but I don't know where to start."

Your husband answers, "I do, the Internet. Your grandson said he wants to teach *you* how to use it. In the meantime, I've done a little searching. We need to educate ourselves about lifestyle options and what to consider when selecting an option. All the sources say that the first consideration should be the kind of care required. I printed out this list of the needs that Medicare.gov says seniors should consider." He shares the following with his mom:

**Will I need help with the following activities of daily living?**
- Bathing
- Dressing
- Eating
- Using the bathroom, including caring for a catheter or colostomy bag if needed
- Moving into or out of bed, chair, of wheelchair
- Other _____

**Will I need help with these additional services?**
- Preparing meals
- Shopping
- Housework and laundry
- Getting to appointments
- Paying bills and other money matters
- Home maintenance and repairs
- Using the telephone
- Other _____

**Will I need help with the following care?**
- Remembering to take medicines
- Diabetes monitoring
- Using eye drops
- Getting oxygen
- Taking care of colostomy or bladder catheters
- Other _____

"Mom, after you've assessed your current and future needs, you can select a living arrangement that accommodates both your and Dad's needs and an arrangement you can afford. The primary choices for senior housing are in this list." They discuss these options:

- **Senior apartment or retirement community for independent living**—living near your friends again, or at least living near your contemporaries with whom you have your stage of life and lifestyle in common
- **Congregate housing**—independent living in a senior apartment with the added services of custodial or medical care
- **Assisted-living facility**—group housing for people with some disabilities; personal care and supportive services, plus some health care and meals, provided around the clock
- **Board and care**—a small assisted-living facility for ten or fewer people
- **Nursing home**—group housing for those who need skilled nursing care and personal care services; meals provided
- **Continuing-care retirement community**—large complex that offers lifetime care; options ranging from independent living to skilled nursing home care

- **Emerging alternatives**—for example, the Green Houses founded by Dr. William H. Thomas and described in an increasing number of publications, along with other alternatives being proposed these days.

The costs of these arrangements vary, of course, from state to state. The more care, the greater the cost. According to the MetLife Mature Market Institute, the average annual cost for a room in an assisted-living facility in 2005 was $34,860, compared with $64,240 for a semiprivate room and $74,095 for a private room in a nursing home. From 2004 to 2005 the cost of assisted-living increased 15.1%, and 5% for nursing-home care. As a generalization, it's best to age in the South—if not for other reasons, for the reason that assisted-living and nursing-home care are substantially cheaper south of the border (the one drawn in the 1860s, that is).

Now the reality is—and forgive the intrusion of a rude reality—if your parents can't afford any of these options, there are others. Medicaid pays for these options only if your parents have depleted their assets. Or your parents can move in with you. If they do, you can hire a home health aide at the 2005 average hourly rate of $19, or you can provide the care yourselves. The National Council on Aging notes that 21 percent of caregivers live in the same household as their care recipient, and 73 percent of the caregivers are women.

If your parents move into your home, retired Superwoman can change the prevailing assumption that women are the better caregivers. The scales of responsibility and showing love for parents need to be balanced. Your workplace outlawed sexual discrimination. The same should be applied to all levels of care for your shared parents.

### Customer Service
*Prepare and Empower while Continuing to Monitor Progress*

Your husband says to his dad, "I'll be glad to go with you to trade your old gas-guzzler in for that hybrid, but we'll need your automobile title. Just grab that and we're off."

Your father-in-law responds, "I can't remember where I put it. I'll look in my desk and filing cabinet . . . Nope, not there. Maybe it's in our safe-deposit box. That must be where it is."

Your husband asks, "OK, is your safe-deposit box at SunTrust or Wachovia?"

Your father-in-law answers, "I'm not sure. It's one or the other."

Your husband says, "Well, just get the key and we'll go to both banks."

Your father-in-law replies, "I'll look for it. It's in my shoeshine drawer, in my cuff-links box, or maybe it's where your mother keeps the silver or her jewelry. Let's ask your mother. She knows."

Your mother-in-law responds, "How should I know where the safe-deposit key is? Your father always took care of that stuff."

Your husband says, "I think it's important for you to know where your things are. We're not trying to tell you what to do. We're trying to empower you to be in charge of your lives. There are several important documents that need to be where you can find them. They also need to be where we can find them if you can't. Let's tackle this document issue together. We're doing the same thing. Let's put together a list of what you need to have on hand and what we, as your trusted loved ones, need to know how to find in a fireproof safe or safe-deposit box." They discuss this list:

- **Living will, aka health care directive**—states your wishes concerning life support or your right to die if you are permanently comatose

- **Durable power of attorney for health care**—empowers a person you designate to be your surrogate in end-of-life care decisions if you are in a permanent coma or painful terminal illness (in some states the living will and the durable power of attorney for health care are combined into what's called an advance health care directive)
- **Durable power of attorney for asset management**—gives someone you trust the ability to make financial decisions for you (be aware, though, that more and more financial institutions are requiring their own forms, and many require reauthorization every six months)
- **Legal will or trust**—tells who inherits your assets; otherwise, the state decides
- **Insurance policies**—life, health, long-term care, homeowners, automobile, and so on
- **Deed(s)**
- **Automobile title(s)**
- **Safe-deposit box location and key**
- **Bank accounts**
- **Credit cards**
- **Household inventory** (particularly of expensive items)
- **Miscellaneous important papers**—birth and marriage certificates, records of military service, passports, health records, tax records (keep tax returns forever), bank statements and cancelled checks (keep for seven years)

Now you have helped your husband hone his skills in giving and getting love in his relationship with his parents. He has learned to accept the responsibility of role reversal in a way that maintains their dignity and aims for their long-term independence. They're the top layer of the boomers' intergenerational sandwich. What about the bottom layer of the father lion's pride?

## CHALLENGE
### Gen-Xers? Millennials? What They Really Are Is Boomer Babies

Speaking of pride—let's not forget those inscrutable offspring of early boomers. You know, those little darlings who declared before they became teenagers (that is, before age nine), "I want to be just like my dad!" A year or two later they complained, "Oh, please, don't lecture me on how I should be like you!" These offspring gained their generational title, Generation X, in 1991 after Douglas Coupland's novel by the same name. This was, by the way, a quarter of a century *after* their conception—and not only that, it was after the boomer population had begotten even the millennial generation.

Just goes to show how our me-generation kept the focus on ourselves. Our children, we thought, owed their identity to us. That's why we have conveniently lumped both the Gen-X and millennial generations under the title *echo boomers*. Who are they, anyway, but boomer babies?

Either the media defined them or they defined the media, but there's no denying that echo boomers were brought up on (some say *by*) television, Atari, and personal computers. Echo boomers are incapable of being shocked or offended. For Generation X and millenials, happiness begins with a C: computer, cell, car, credit card. The money they spend on more minutes or more memory is not discretionary. It's subsistence spending (and it can always go on their credit cards). They have an arcane definition of *friend* that only their contemporaries comprehend. Its meaning is probably derived from a contextual clue, inflection, or some sort of non-verbal messaging. At any rate, their boomer parents have gleaned that the Gen-X "friend" means anybody from colleague to lover, real or virtual. Try as we do, boomers never get it right, so we avoid the term, unless we know we're on solid ground by using it to refer to their computer.

Echo boomers are in constant, instant contact with their real and virtual friends via cell phone, instant messaging, or e-mail. Typically, the caller begins a conversation with the highly profound and urgent "What's up?" To which the friend responds, "Not much." Gen X-ers and their millennial followers consider their computers, cell phones, cars, and credit cards an entitlement. It's ironic that these generations are deemed spoiled by our babyboom generation. Boomers gave them these things because . . . well, for the best reason there is—their friends had them.

In contrast to the infamous generation gap between us and our parents, we generally have harmonious relationships with our echo-boomer offspring. We vowed to be "friends forever" with our kids because we remember how disconnected our parents were from us. This vow meant we would adopt their lingo, at least in conversations with them: "Like, like, well, like yeah, you know, I'm with ya." We adopted their clothes. Of particular note is the tight white T-shirt, showing—never mind what it showed of the boomer. We pride ourselves in our affirmation of their lifestyle choices: the stay-at-home dad, the job-hopper, the opposite-sex roommate "friend," the boomerang who returns home after the roommate relationship dissolves. We even drink their libation of choice, super mocha café latté. We accept their nocturnal social structure, defined as groups (some say packs) that make plans via their cell phones at 11:55 p.m. for whatever they will do from midnight to 3 a.m.

They may never thank us for it, but Gen-Xers and millennials are the beneficiaries of causes the boom generation fought for, namely civil rights and Title IX. The reason for "colored" water fountains before the 1960s is *inconceivable* to them. "Was the water dyed red or blue?" they ask. And that little darling of ours who declared, "I want to be just like my dad" was a girl. She could aspire to be a track-and-field champion while majoring in electrical engineering.

For our part, we boomers need to give up living our lives *again* through our kids. It's time to graduate from the parent peer pressure that pitted us against other moms and dads for perfect parenting status. Our parenting mantra was "Leave no hint of potential untapped," as if our children were a cradle-to-college project in product development. We made the world their oyster. How could it be otherwise, when übermom was mother-of-pearl?

I know, I know. They did it all themselves. That's what we say because we've been living vicariously through them. They're adults now. They want to find their own purpose and make their generational mark. We may be nostalgic about the 1950s and '60s, but don't expect your echo boomer to be. "C'mon, Mom," your twenty-something says, "You wouldn't *really* want to go back to that ignorant pre–Rosa Parks era, those boring summers before Sputnik when kids had nothing to do but sell lemonade and lie in the hammock, and those horribly sad 1960s when everybody was getting assassinated or turning on and dropping out. Besides, nobody had computers or cells back then."

Dare you, just dare you tell your Gen-Xer that Steve Jobs and Bill Gates are boomers? (Yup, both born in 1955.) That Bill Gates probably achieved what he did because his mother was a super-woman? That the Internet was conceived by visionary thinking in the 1960s, what Gen-Xers think of as those "sad, pot-smoking '60s"? Don't bother. The millennial generation hardly remembers dial-up. For all the younger of them know, human knowledge began with the Web. They think God created heaven and earth and then there was Google.

## STRATEGY

### Network Gen-Xers, Millennials, and Their Grandparents!

Besides everything else boomers did for them, our children should know that they're the beneficiaries of the digital age. We were the Robespierres and Thomas Paines of the information technology revolution. Our generation was the last to be born BC, before computers. Most of us learned e-mail, Internet searching, and sundry software programs on the job. We were part of the coup de grâce that replaced paper-and-pencil records with computer databases. If we didn't learn at work or while acquiring one of those graduate degrees, we were socially humiliated into learning. Everyone else on the planet—including our children—conversed about their optical mice, their desktops, their laptops. Everyone else could design and print their own invitations and holiday e-letters, do their taxes online, and get the goods from e-stores.

But our parents were long out of the workforce—and peer social force—that drove computer knowledge. Remember that people feel threatened by the unknown. Our parents don't like computers because they've never used them. Compounding their fear is their lack of typing skills. In their generation, typing was something only secretaries and war correspondents did. They resent our chatter that uses all those terms they don't understand. Remember the time your husband boasted about the gigs in his hard drive? "So you're taking Viagra now, are you?" your mother asked as she scowled and shook her head.

"I don't like computers," she continued. "They're to blame for our nest egg getting squashed five years ago—all that technology stuff investors thought was the way to go. And then computers caused all those corporate crimes. Now computers are to blame for—at least partly to blame for—unemployment. Robots are just computers made to look like people, and they shouldn't be putting cars together."

The irony in the elderly (sorry, Mother, I mean *upper crust* of the multigenerational sandwich) avoiding the computer is that it is a wonderful tool for them to use to stay connected. If they can't venture physically, they can venture virtually. For a googol of reasons, computer use helps people stay independent.

Cross the digital divide. The quickest way to validate your echo boomer is through his computer. If you talk computerese, he'll understand you and think you're cool. Why not enlist his expertise to get Grandma and Grandpa cyberconnected? You know your mother won't learn from you or your husband, but she'd love the attention from her grandson. What an opportunity! You regain long-lost intimacy with your son through his computer, your son gets validation of himself through this new role as teacher, and Gram and Gramps become computer savvy—well, at least e-mail and Google functional. And all three generations get connected. It's a stroke of genius.

## CHALLENGE
### Being the Parent of Adult Children Still Means "Do as I Say"

Quick! Before your husband says he wants to be the server, Superwoman reminds him of the objective here: to put the works in that multigenerational sandwich. Second adulthood boomers are the meat in that sandwich, the lynchpin between the generations. This requires the kind of leadership that corporate restructuring taught. It is our responsibility to inspire by example, to foster participation in a cause, not to command and control. This means that Superwoman's husband can be the router; his son should be the server. It's time to defer to his son's greater expertise (and interpersonal skills with Grandma) to accomplish his grandparents' computer literacy.

Your echo boomer will find it validating to be given the control. Your parents will be empowered by gaining a skill giving them more control over their lives. Isn't it ironic that what you want for your parents—their long-term independence—is what you want for your children, too?

If long-term independence is really what you and your husband want for your children, then your husband will have to change his style of parenting. These children of his are grown-ups now, sort of—well, many of them are and the others will get there sooner or later. Just because they're past twenty-one doesn't mean parenting is over. Superwoman knows parenting is never over, at least not until very old age brings a role reversal. She also knows that being the parent of an adult child requires something altogether different from parenting a younger child. Superwoman's husband, however, learned one style of parenting, which he still practices. Essentially, it's "I'm boss; you do as I say."

Before the reengineered workplace taught him otherwise, the boomer man thought leadership meant issuing orders. If your husband still thinks his parental role should be of that style—a style that worked, if he was lucky, until his children were sixteen—he will alienate them and portray himself as an inaccessible, orderbarking autocrat. Again, Superwoman takes the lead in restructuring her husband's outmoded concept of leadership to suit the climate change of parenting adult children.

## STRATEGY
### Validate Your Children as Adults, and Model Twenty-First-Century Second Adulthoods

Unless your children need your active intervention and continued strong hand, all they want from you now is your validation of them as adults. Validation means accepting them for who they are, not as clones of you, not as children you control, and not as people through whom you live vicariously. Superwoman explains to her husband that you both are still parenting in the most significant way you have always parented: you are modeling how to handle life.

Superwoman takes the lead in implementing the change in her husband's parenting style, from autocratic boss to leader inspiring by example. She says, "Honey, it's like *rolling over*. Remember 1956 when Chuck Berry sang 'Roll Over Beethoven,' declaring a new era, the ultimate rock 'n' roll call to arms? Or *rolling over* cell minutes to give them a new start, or rolling over maturing funds into a new issue, or the IRA *rollover?* We're just *rolling over* into a new stage of our parenting.

Our kids are still learning from us, although they'd never admit it. Sure, we'll always be their bridge over troubled water, but they're learning from us a new lesson never before offered by a generation: how to reengineer first adulthood for second adulthood. We're their mentors for a new era in the history of humanity. We're modeling the partnership marriage reengineered for the twenty-first-century second adulthood. Every challenge we accept for the rest of our lives will inspire them when they reach their own second adulthoods. You know they expected us simply to melt into that directionless trip-to-trip routine they imagine retirement as, because they thought we were half in the grave. Well, aren't we showing them! *Showing* them, Honey, not *telling* them anymore."

The world—and our children—have heard enough of our generation's sound and fury. Second-adulthood parenting is our opportunity to signify something for the next generation. The greatest thing we can do for our children now is to empower them to be responsible adults by modeling what that means. Being the meat in the intergenerational sandwich means giving responsibility to earlier and later generations. For our kids it means showing them that we can succeed in a new and long era of second-adulthood parenting—by parenting by example. Now we can be mellow with our kids. It's as if Olivia Newton-John were singing to us in a new context, thirty years after we first heard "Have You Never Been Mellow?"

*Have you never been happy just to hear your song?*
*Have you never let someone else be strong?*

Your song are those wonderful children you created and nurtured. Now you have to let go and let them find their own strength.

## OBJECTIVE 5

## Go for the Gold and Silver
### (What Friends Want)

Question: If you could choose, which of the following would you want more than anything else in the world?
   a) the latest model Lincoln Navigator with all the bells and whistles
   b) a house twice the size of the one you have now and with an indoor pool and gym
   c) the love and respect of friends

The typical boomer would answer, "Why do I have to choose? I want them all. Besides, I already have friends, and if I had the Navigator and estate home, I'd have more friends."

## CHALLENGE
### The Value of a Friend Equals His Home's Square Footage

The boom-generation ethos goes something like this:

- I believe in hard work because it rewards me with money. The more money I make, the more successful I am. I prove my success through what I own. The more I own, the more evidence of success I have.
- I believe in competition. To prove I am more successful than others, I buy and display more than others. My conspicuous display of wealth garners friendship because people admire me for my success. In fact, my self-worth is whatever I display as my net worth.
- Others accept me based on the same criteria I apply to myself, and my friends share my values.
- Therefore, my friends like me for my stuff.

Not exactly a classic Greek syllogism, but it does show how boomers got the reputation for equating everything to money—including the friends they say they *value*.

Now answer this question: Who said of Americans that their pursuit of prosperity is a "restless, burning passion that increases with satisfaction"?

a) Herbert Hoover in 1928
b) Allen Greenspan in 2005
c) Alexis de Tocqueville in 1835
d) Jimmy Carter in 1981

Oh, how Gen X would love to answer Greenspan or Carter and plant the roots of boomer materialism in our generation! Actually, Alexis de Tocqueville said this in 1835, attributing Americans' unquenchable desire for things to the mores of American democracy. We are demonstrating an *enculturated national DNA.*

The notion that Americans inherited their acquisitive nature is getting support from another national trait: we're risk takers. Regardless of when our ancestors transplanted themselves into our culture, they had to risk predictability for the sake of promise. This risk taking is what put our country at the top of the heap in less than 200 years of existence. But risk taking also involves self-interest, commitment to a personal vision, and sacrifice for the reward at the end of the tunnel—or the rainbow. Any way you look at it, this reward was wealth. In 1928, by the way, Herbert Hoover promised "a car in every garage" along with that chicken in every pot.

So what's at play here? Have boomers gotten a bum rap? Partly. We didn't invent the system nor the psyche that equates every-thing—even friendship—with the bottom line. If you believe in enculturated national DNA, you could say we inherited the genes for it, sort of like a dollar-sign birthmark on our forehead—or in the palm of our right hand, the one we shake with.

At the same time, there's a nurture part to the equation, a part we can't blame on inheritance. Sometime between Watergate and the death knell of the Equal Rights Amendment, boomers gave up their causes and headed for Wall Street. Progress became defined by what and how much we consumed, not by what we did for oth-ers. We read F. Scott Fitzgerald's *The Great Gatsby* but missed the point: that you can't buy love or friendship. Instead, we built our McMansions and furnished them in a day with Rooms-to-Go in socially correct shades from café au lait to not-quite-white. When we upped a notch or wanted a change, we had an estate sale and started over again with a bigger house. Our homes reflect our val-ues—and the depth of our friendships.

If friendship really can be bought, then it might as well be out-sourced. We might as well pay a therapist or bribe our children. But wait! We can change this! And who's in charge of our life anyway? If you say, "Superwoman," then you're on the right track, the track to a second-adulthood redemption from our money-buys-even-friendship mentality. And this is redemption in the sense of changing for the better. Redemption begins with the prefix *re-*, which means "again" or "anew," as in more than 450 words in *Webster's New Collegiate Dictionary,* from *reachieve* to *rewire.* Let's use *re-* words! Besides, Americans love redemption. We believe in second, third, and fourth chances. That's why we look at the boomers' second adulthood as a second chance at life. Let's do it right this time. Under Superwoman's guidance, we will retool our criteria for friendship and embrace the Joneses instead of keeping up with them.

## CHALLENGE
### It's All About Me = My Friends Meet My Needs

Hold on, Superwoman. You can't take your entire generation by the scruff of the neck and shake out its shabby net-worth criteria for friendship. Not yet, at least. There's another challenge to be addressed first. And—you guessed it—it's a male thing. In a word, it's that exasperating, irritating, calculating, agitating, maddening, and infuriating self-focus. It's been said (by everyone but the boomer male) that the boomer male never got the word that astronomy evicted him from his place at the center of the universe *centuries* before 1946.

The male of just about every species is self-focused. Back in the cave days when primal women were focused on their babies' welfare, the men were out proving to one another that they were the fittest in survival competition. Then they'd come home and communicate their superiority by beating their chests. And this was how manhood was defined—by other men. The women just sighed and tolerated it.

## CHALLENGE
### Boomer Men Can't Let Go of Their Inner Cowboy

Fast-forward to continental destiny. When it came to American masculinity, men defined themselves as the conquerors of the wild frontier or the heroes in cowboy-and-Indian sagas. In fairness, though, boomer men have had a tough time with what's masculine because its definition has changed three times since World War II. That's because women—finally—had a say-so. Somehow through these redefinitions of manhood, however, the American male has continued to stay self-focused. Amazing.

First-wave boomer men grew up with John Wayne's and Ernest Hemingway's protagonists as role models for manhood. The standard they set for masculinity demanded a visceral confrontation with an adversary. Manhood was defined in the struggle, not necessarily in the victory. In the end, the hero just "saddled up" or heroically waited for death. If that hero wanted a woman, he dragged her across town and threw her into bed, like taming the shrew. Otherwise, women were just cardboard backdrops to the drama of men going after what they wanted. It was two men, of course, Fats Waller and Andy Razaf, who wrote the lyrics and music to "Find Out What They Like and How They Like It." The refrain describes that era's idea of how women held onto a man:

> *Find out what they like, and how they like it,*
> *And let 'em have it just that way.*
> *Give 'em what they want and when they want it,*
> *Without a single word to say.*

The woman's movement and flower-child culture of the 1960s threw out this machismo, at least in theory. Everybody was supposed to get in touch with their inner something. That was fine and dandy for boomer women, but most boomer men just couldn't let go of their inner bullfighter or their inner John Wayne.

Navel-gazing was something the American male simply didn't do, unless it was gazing at a navel on someone of the opposite sex.

Now men are admonished to connect with their feminine side. No way is the boomer male going to embrace his feminine side! "I'll leave that," he says, "to the millennial metrosexuals or the girlie men." You'll just have to deal with it, superwomen, your husbands will never let go of their inner cowboy. Too bad. Chest beating never impressed *real* women. Why don't men get it? Only Hollywood's Jane and the jungle were conquered by Tarzan, a fiction of men.

Boomer standards of masculinity were—and remain—for their fellow males. This affects how they relate to one another and how they form friendships. Subliminally, at least, it's still "who's top dog" or the better "inner warrior." Oh, well . . .

Lucky for your hubby he had you in his first adulthood! Thanks to Superwoman's multitasking, he only had to handle his job and half the parenting—and oh yes, his golf game. Now he's retired. "Where are all my friends?" he wonders. Besides the daily structure and sense of purpose his job gave him, it also supplied his friends—sort of.

His co–child-rearing days provided his other source of friends—sort of. During those decades his friends were the fathers of his children's friends. His hardwired male boomer competitiveness carried over to his relationships with these fathers. These "friendships" were based on two forms of one-upmanship (a socially correct way of saying his primal need to conquer). The first form was rooted in your husband's vicarious identity with his child, particularly the male child. Through his son's sports, your husband was vicariously competing with other fathers.

The second form of one-upmanship was comparing notes with other boomer males about where they were and what they were doing during the major milestones of human history, defined as that period between 1946 and 1964. The conversation went something like this:

"I'm Steve's dad. I think I met you last summer at the state tennis finals." (*I'm facing off for a male friendship.*)

"That couldn't have been me because Keith was playing for his Southeastern ranking in Nashville. What is Steve's ranking?" (*I'm superior, but I'll take him on anyway.*)

"Steve is 22nd in the 16s. He also plays singles for Wesley Academy. We won state last year. How about Keith?" (*I'm a worthy opponent/potential friend. I'll compete.*)

"Keith is ranked 18 in the Southeast. He plays for Middleton Academy when he's not playing in national competition. He got to quarterfinals in Kansas City last summer. The scouts from Purdue were there. I think they have their eye on him." (*He's no competition. I've won.*)

(*He's won. I'll change to a subject I know I'm superior in. I'll take this friendship competition to the next level.*) "I was watching the Purdue-Indiana game when Cassius Clay first announced he was the greatest. Remember that?"

"I sure do. Greatest boxer there ever was—or ever will be. You ever boxed?" (*I've got him—again! Let's see how he answers this one.*)

(*Aha, we have something very important in common. I like this man. But how do I answer the ultimate male question of whether I ever boxed? Oh, for God's sake, Ernest Hemingway, my hero, boxed. But I have to be honest.*) "No, but I played football for Auburn. I missed playing against Joe Namath by a couple of years. Remember that '69 Super Bowl game? Greatest game in the history of football. They just don't make players like Namath anymore." (*I wonder how he'll respond to this.*)

"I played a little football, but I gave up sports to work with Reverend King in Selma. Just had to after James Meredith was wounded by that sniper. And right out of college I got drafted to 'Nam. Hardest time this country has ever seen—or ever will again." (*I've just given him the ultimate boomer résumé. Let's hear him top this one.*)

"You know, our kids think we were all at Woodstock or Haight-Ashbury in '69, but everybody I know was in 'Nam, at Ray Charles's concerts, or watching Armstrong and Aldrin walk on the moon. Funny, isn't it?" (*I give up. He wins. He's worthy competition; therefore, we're friends.*)

That's about it for your husband's first-adulthood friends. Now that he's off the career treadmill and empty nested, he wonders, "Where are my friends?" Superwoman knows. Superwoman knows because friendships have always been important to her because . . . well, she's a woman.

If Superwoman is going to get this partnership marriage off to its new frontier, she'll have to help her husband achieve this last transition objective. You know, the one you learned in kindergarten: "Make new friends but keep the old. One is silver and the other gold."

## STRATEGY

### Use Interpersonal Skills—From Aristotle's Definitions of Friendship to the New Paradigm

Your husband probably assumes that your ability to make friends is a woman's secret, a special magnetism that women share and that is denied to men. Whatever. The problem is that you can't teach your husband the friendship-garnering intuition, empathy, and sensitivity skills endowed to you by nature and nurture. Men need the logical, the rational, the left-brain methodology. Baby-boomer men who professionally matured in the corporate reengineering milieu learned that adapting to change was a survivor skill. Hence, they are accustomed to a strategy that defines a problem and outlines an action plan to implement positive change.

## The Problem

Try to define the problem in corporate restructuring lingo—for instance, "Honey, it's like the corporate climate has changed, and we have to change with it. Remember one of the warning signs that corporate change is needed? It's needed when management is still committed to 1955 but it's the twenty-first century. That's the problem here. Your friends [sort-of friends] came with your job and our kids."

He realizes this. He also now realizes that because he relied on you to arrange social engagements, most of your marriage's friends are your friends. Beyond what he has in common with his golf buddy, your husband doesn't know how to cultivate new friendships or nourish old ones.

It is Superwoman's *obligation* to teach him. What if you should predecease him? You want him to have a fulfilling life with or without you. You think it's healthy for your relationship to have independent friendships. (Besides, you don't like golf.) And he can't assume that he can count on relatives—not even siblings—just because they're relatives. Remember the old saying: Friends are the relatives you choose. A ten-year study at Flinders University in Australia showed that those who had a network of good friends and confidants outlived by 22 percent those with the fewest friends.

## Aristotle as Outside Consultant

Superwoman realizes she can't reengineer her husband's friendship skills in-house. It just won't work for you to say to him, "Honey, here's the way women do it. Just copy me." She realizes she has to call in an outside consultant to assess the problem and formulate a plan to deal with it.

Reengineering also taught you to look within the company for the people who have the skills and experience to help implement the paradigm shift after the plan is formulated. Therefore, you and your husband need to be part of the consulting team. Your husband will be responsible for implementing and sustaining the changes called for by the team's assessment. You will act as mentor to employees needing retraining (you know who that will be). The consultant from the outside is Aristotle, an expert in friendship.

Following this strategy, Superwoman calls in Aristotle as consultant. His assessment confirms the challenges that our me-generation has with friendships. Aristotle explains the distinctions among three kinds of friendship: utility, pleasure, and virtue. Friendships of *utility* are based on what my friend can do for me. These are the friendships your husband had at work. Friendships of *pleasure* are based on the fun or entertainment a friend offers me. These are the golf-buddy friendships or those developed during vicarious competition through the kids' sports.

Aristotle pauses to explain that friendships of utility or pleasure last only as long as the circumstances that gave rise to them. This explains why your husband found himself friendless after he retired and the kids left home. Friendships of utility and pleasure are also me-focused because these friends are not loved for themselves but for what they can provide in advantage or pleasure. Once these friends are no longer useful or fun, the friendships dissolve.

The third form of friendship, Aristotle says, is what we should all strive for. This is perfect friendship—friendship of *virtue*. Friendship on this level assumes the inherent goodness of both friends' characters. Aristotle says this goodness is a necessary precondition to attaining a relationship based on mutual admiration.

Friends sharing this perfect relationship wish good for one another for their friend's sake and not for what pleasure or usefulness the friend affords. But, of course, perfect friendships are also useful and pleasurable. Examples of these friendships are rare because few people can attain this ideal: Crito's friendship with Socrates, Plato's with Aristotle, Jefferson's with Madison, and a woman's friendship with at least three other women.

### Implementing and Sustaining the Friendship Paradigm Shift

Now your husband knows why his (sort-of) friends have disappeared. But how does Superwoman help him cultivate new friendships and sustain old ones in his changed circumstances—in his retirement? You tell him that his transition to second adulthood is analogous to the transition he made from the pre-global manager to new manager-leader. The old-style manager was boss, with a big, bad, formidable *B*. The corporate restructuring he experienced in the 1980s taught him to become a team leader who fosters—not bosses—participation. The transition required sensitivity training and involved learning the skills women are born with. The skills were and are called (nonsexually connotative) *interpersonal skills* as a sop to men because men were already on their guard with women breaking glass ceilings in the workplace. The skills might as well have been called *women's innate skills*. But a lot of transitions were going on, and women were willing to concede on this one.

The point here is that Superwoman is the in-house mentor in her husband's learning these interpersonal skills, the same skills essential to cultivating and sustaining friendships. In short, it's axiomatic to women: To have a friend, you have to be a friend. In his poem "Tintern Abbey" Wordsworth referred to ". . . that best portion of a good man's life, / His little, nameless, unremembered, acts / Of kindness and of love." Basically, friendship is in the specifics of the acts. Your husband can overcome his male handicap in this area by learning the skills essential to kindness and love and then watching you practice them:

- Giving time
- Keeping promises
- Demonstrating loyalty
- Showing concern
- Expressing gratitude
- Avoiding comparisons
- Forgiving and apologizing

These acts of kindness and love require a focus on others. Yes, sociologists say we have a (hardwired) self-preservation need to be heard and to have our needs met by others. The self-absorbed, I'm-so-busy boomers have taken the need to be heard to another level—the level that has earned for them the me-generation label.

We have cultivated the habit, for example, of beginning conversations with "I need your input." Usually this is a disguised way of saying, "I want confirmation of my opinion." When our listener tries to express his opinion (his "input"), we interrupt him midway through sentences because we're not listening to what he says. When our listener gropes for words to express his thoughts, we respond with hurry-it-up-already gestures and proceed with a speech that sounds like we're running for office.

A relationship that is always taking and never giving is not friendship. We fool ourselves if we call it friendship, just like we fool ourselves when we call a cell phone tower a pine tree because it's disguised as one. The genuine, the sincere, always trumps show. Again, it's about empathetic communication. This ability— or skill, because it *can* be learned—is prerequisite to friendship.

In addition to these friendship skills are two lofty requisites for perfect friendship: wishing good for your friend and sharing a common purpose. A friendship of virtue is a sublime gift achieved only by those who are willing to give of themselves and get the gift in return. It is the kind of friendship we all should strive for. Aristotle says that this level of friendship is possible only when two people have the time to achieve intimacy. That's the payoff (sorry, but boomers just think in these terms) of your second adulthood. Your husband now has the time to achieve this level of friendship in shared common purpose. This is the first opportunity for you and your husband to redeem your me-generation reputation. Opportunities await you in the new goals you are about to achieve.

PART FOUR

# Reengineering Your Lifestyle

SO FAR SUPERWOMAN HAS DEALT with retirement adaptations that are problematic for men. She has helped her husband find a new identity in his real time of retirement. He has learned to be the luckiest person in the world by reengineering his relationship skills. He is practicing the empathetic communication that Superwoman taught him for giving and getting love in his relationships with her, his parents, and his kids. Superwoman has also taught him how to enrich existing friendships and cultivate new ones. Now you both are ready to be all that you can be—and haven't been in your first adulthood. If your second adulthood is to redefine the human experience, you've got to start with the body you'll need to get there. But before you can "just do it" you'll have to get over several obstacles—strike that, challenges—to your boomer body re-generation.

## OBJECTIVE 6

## Learn from First Adulthood

### (Morph That Body into a New Form)

Boomers rule. In fact, boomers have ruled since 1993. That's when President William J. Clinton took over leadership of the most powerful country in the world. After eight years he was followed by President George W. Bush. Both these leaders were born in 1946. Not only do they represent the pros and cons of American values, they also embody—quite literally—boomers' debates with their bodies. Regardless of where we are in our own debate, we can draw inspiration from these two body winners.

In 2004 a quadruple bypass jumpstarted Bill Clinton's new lifestyle. Several years earlier his cholesterol and weight had testified to his eating habits. Ironically, Dr. Dean Ornish, consultant to Clinton in 1999, vocally advocated lifestyle changes in diet and exercise to avert the coronary artery disease that leads to half a million bypass surgeries a year. Obviously, Clinton didn't listen. But remember the redemption? Now Clinton feels ready to take on his second adulthood *with vigor*. He said in a presurgery interview, "Some of this is genetic, and I may have done some damage in those years when I was too careless about what I ate. So for whatever reason, I've got a problem, and I've got a chance to deal with it." And deal with it he has—eschewing those French fries and making his heart "pump iron."

Then there's George W. Bush. Long ago he conquered his potentially destructive love of drink. Determined to make exercise part of his lifestyle, he gave up the track for the trail when osteoarthritis halted his running regimen. Now he bicycles with the best of them—indeed, with the very best of them, Lance Armstrong.

When Henry Kissinger said, "The task of a leader is to take his people from where they are to where they have not been," he wasn't talking about wellness choices. But what could be more meaningful for our generation than adopting healthy, sustainable lifestyle choices that will assure our fitness for twenty-first-century second adulthoods? What could be more meaningful for future generations than following our lead? We ask, though, who is the leader who will take us to where we have not been? Will it be the USDA or the diet gurus or the latest and greatest antiaging miracle? Who do you think? Superwoman.

Superwoman has a vision for her generation's new direction. Like the best corporate leaders, she will inspire by example and empower the members of her generation to make lifestyle decisions for themselves (as Clinton and Bush, both married to superwomen, made the decisions for themselves . . . hmm?). Regardless of where you and your husband are on the need-to-change spectrum, now is the time to weigh in on the rest of your lives—those potentially long, healthy, and productive second adulthoods. You'd better believe that Clinton and Bush don't intend to spend their second adulthoods in rocking chairs watching the world go by! They're reengineering their bodies for their re-generation.

## CHALLENGE
### I Have All the Answers to Eternal Youth and Good Health

Why, oh why, would we fall for a pill, spray, or patch that claims to—

- reduce body fat and build lean muscle without exercise or dieting,
- improve cognitive, immune, and sexual functions,
- remove wrinkles and cellulite,
- recover hair color and strength,
- and turn back the body's biological time clock ten to twenty years?

We did—to the tune of $70 million! The product was HGH (Human Growth Hormone) Enhancer. The same quacks also deceptively marketed Fat Blaster, Super Carb Blocker, and Ultimate Wild Oregano Oil before the FTC caught up with them and ordered them to pay $20 million in consumer redress. The charlatans had undertaken such an audaciously bold, in-our-face Internet, television, and radio advertising scam because they knew their target market: you, me—yup, all us seventy-seven million narcissistic, forever-young boomers, presently aged in our early forties to sixty. We control 50 percent of the country's gross domestic product, and we go after just about anything that promises more boom for our bucks. The marketing industry knows darn well it won't hook us by marketing to our chronological age. They're aware that first-wave boomers especially have a cognitive, or perceived, age that is decades behind their chronological age; they know that some of us will dwell in the 1960s forever. Boomers, as a matter of fact, have numerous ages just as valid as chronological age; we have our feel age, our look age, our do age, our interest age, and so on. And that's good—as long as we're aware that over-the-counter or Internet-vended antiaging miracle treatments, otherwise known as snake oil, are unregulated by the FDA. Yet these antiaging miracle treatments are a multibillion-dollar industry targeted at us, and we buy the miracle because . . . well, because we want to believe in the miracle.

In buying the miracle, we believe we have all the answers to eternal youth and good health. Why not? We control everything else. We're products of the 1960s zeitgeist that first articulated—for the Western world, at least—the interconnectedness of mind, body, and spirit. With this New Age weltanschauung came our thinking that we are the cause of every effect, which translates into a mentality, at one extreme, of blaming the victim (of disease, condition, etc.), and at the other extreme, of "it's all my doing" (good health, good looks, etc.). This mind-set has led to our generation's guilt about or obsession with our body form, its facade, and its health destiny.

But what good is guilt without a solution to the problem causing it? It's no good. So we've invented the solutions—mostly the miracle cures or nanosecond quick fixes because we're used to quick fixes and because we didn't ever have to do much the really hard way like our parents did. We think we did, or at least we tell our kids we did. But we really didn't. It's no wonder we make millionaires of the charlatans who promise no-sweat, overnight svelte. And we convince ourselves—when we want to indulge our guilt—that we don't know what's in that box of chocolates.

There's another problem that compounds our dealing with the reality confronting us (sagging faces, corpulent bodies, HDL vs. LDL). It's the feeling we have that we're just not in the know, and the resentment we harbor for those who claim they are. We baby boomers started the health food craze when we were making love and smoking marijuana. Somehow the antiwar movement got connected to organically grown vegetables and tofu. We can always blame or credit California—depending on which side of the meat market you're on.

What we've got today is an extreme segment of the population—California grown, but organically spread to the rest of our continent—that believes they're physically, mentally, and spiritually superior because they eat—or don't eat—certain foods. Now sales of natural and organic foods are growing at an 18 percent annual rate and surpassed $17 billion in 2002. Going vegan and eating only organic have become status habits of those of us who smugly embrace the "secrets" of health and longevity. If you can't tell your dinner host that there are at least half a dozen foods you "can't eat," you're unrefined—like the only kind of sweetener you use. (But there's a nemesis lurking here: PCBs and mercury contaminate that fountain of youth!)

So, if we're so smart and so in control, why are most of us overweight and out of shape?

## CHALLENGE
### Calorie In, Calorie Out or On—It's Just Too Easy for the Boomer Mind

It's the calories, stupid. Why can't we get it? Healthy, sustainable weight loss stems from eating a balanced diet and burning up more calories than we consume. The 60 percent of us who are overweight or obese need to get with this elegantly simple program *now*. But we don't. Is it just too easy for the boomer mind? Or is it some penchant for hocus-pocus in the mitochondria we inherited from Eve?

Poor food choices began in the Garden of Eden. As Mark Twain had it, Adam would've eaten the serpent if the serpent had been forbidden. Maybe we need to forbid sound nutrition and exercise. Less than two centuries ago, ladies ate arsenic wafers to achieve the Victorian ideal of pale complexions. No fear now. We have nutritionists, MDs, the CDC, the FDA, the American Diabetes Association, the American Heart Association, and the American Cancer Society, to name a few, looking after us. They tell us what to eat and what not to eat. Disappointingly, their advice seems to change monthly, and this year's advice can debunk last year's.

Less than a decade ago athletes and weekend warriors—that was us, remember?—were urged to consume lots of pasta for endurance. Now pasta—unless it's whole-grain, and who eats whole-grain fettuccine?—is tantamount to junk food. Remember when eggs were shunned as the number one cholesterol culprit responsible for heart disease? For decades there was nothing redeeming about the egg unless it was hatched into a low-fat chicken. Now eggs are incredibly edible again—a complete protein, replete with vitamins A and $B_{12}$, folic acid, and riboflavin— and three a week are recommended. Even real men eat quiche now. Do we have the final word on coffee yet? Currently it's an antioxidant and, therefore, it's good for us but check again next week.

The surprise miracle food of 2005 was dark chocolate. If you're a properly educated—or rather a lifelong—learner of what's nutritious, you know these things. Chocolate was discovered to have flavonoids and epicatechins, which are antioxidants. (How many of these terms are in your repertoire? Look up *flavonoid* and you learn that it's "a large group of plant substances that includes anthocyanins." OK, how could you be so stupid?) These whatever-they-are, we're told, lower blood pressure and decrease the number of free radicals in the body. (You *do* know what free radicals are, of course. They've been around for a couple of years.) To prove these miraculous, newfound properties of chocolate, thirteen (significant number choice here) volunteers were given chocolates in daily *doses* (this is a medical experiment, not an epicurean's nirvana) for two weeks. These chocolates were in a form the everyday American consumer encounters, that is, laden with saturated fat and plucked from a box with a beautiful bow. After two weeks of deliciously lowered blood pressure and decreased free radicals from nearly seven thousand dark-chocolate calories, the volunteers were deemed more susceptible to heart disease because of their saturated fat consumption. Duh! Anyone for straight cocoa? How about adding the latest carcinogenic artificial sweetener and soy milk? Thank you, I'll wait for the pill.

The mid-2005 herbal *wunder*-remedies ginkgo biloba and St. John's wort are now considered no better than placebos. Cinnamon and curry anyone? Got blood clots—or vampires? Try garlic. Omega-3 fatty acids are supergood for the heart as long as you don't eat much of the fish that have it, since they are replete with mercury, which increases the risk of heart disease.

Just when you think you have all the food villains en brochette, a new one emerges. General Mills had hardly exchanged its processed grains for unprocessed ones when another cereal killer was identified: the tasteless, odorless, but heart-lethal trans fat. Oh, remember the good ole days—when you were in college— when fat was fat, and fat was bad, and that was that? Now there's good fat, bad fat, and very bad fat. And they all have lots of calories. Vegetable and olive oils—good fats—have 120 calories per tablespoon. One of the bad fats, butter, has 100 calories per tablespoon. The 2005 Food Pyramid recommends two tablespoons of the 120-calorie-per-tablespoon kind. Choose your fat wisely.

The same is true for carbohydrates. The good ones get the orange-colored (if you're not color-blind like 10 percent of our male population) slice of the 2005 Pyramid. Good carbohydrates are the ones that testify to the don't-mess-with-Mother-Nature, brown-is-good new axiom for grains. We're told by the MyPyramid.gov Web site that white is bad, or at least a waste of our daily allotted calories.

Ah, but here is where you can be as smart as your organic, whole-food friends: when it comes to calories, sugar is sugar is sugar even if it sounds healthier as *organic whole cane sugar, turbinado, high-fructose corn syrup,* or any other of its forty-some aliases. One teaspoon of any of them is 15 calories. From a calorie standpoint, one could logically ask why we are *supposed* to eat 240 calories of oils and none in sugar (beyond what's naturally in milk and fruit). The USDA says we eat twenty teaspoons of sugar a day, and that's twenty teaspoons too much. Sugar doesn't even have a color on the pyramid. If you are what you eat, why not sweet? Oh, well . . .

There's also the conspiracy theory behind the American diet. We get a little suspicious when we're told that by eating the right foods we're acting as our own environmental protection agency. And that new Pyramid that took four years and $2.4 million to produce? (Quick, tell me what food is blue. Maybe Dan Brown and Indiana Jones can get together and unlock the Pyramid's code.) The Pyramid is in code; it's a cybersecret. You can go online and figure it out yourself. This suspicion is underlined by our mass media throwing out terms that probably even the Surgeon General would have to look up. Words like the following:

| perillyl alcohol | glutathione |
| quercetin | limonoids |
| phytochemicals | genistein |
| idoles | sulforaphane |
| polyphenols | ellagic acid |
| lignan | zeaxanthin (my favorite because it ends in "thin") |

We get ads from reputable sources (we think) that tout the latest five-hundred-page guide to miracle foods that heal everything and erase fat. We think we've finally found the fountain of youth when we see that eight of the dozen editorial advisors are MD's and the others are PhD's or PharmD's. We thumb through the sixty-page ad booklet, and we read *amazing breakthrough, secret nutrient, missing link, thin person's secret, magic mineral, foods that keep you cancer-free, ultimate weight-loss food, calorie-blocker food.* So many wows!

Then we read that this guide will tell us about the food that enabled Scarlett O'Hara and so many other Southern belles to maintain narrow waists. Well, we may not know as much as the experts about nutrition, but we do know that the South has the biggest girth of the country and that a *corset* maintained Scarlett O'Hara's seventeen-inch waist. Besides, after Tara was destroyed by the Yankees, she vowed, "As God is my witness, I'll never be hungry again!" She would've given up her tiny waist for one potato and declared that this $37.95 guide to miracle foods wasn't worth a hill of beans. Unsolicited Internet advertising isn't called *spam* for nothing.

From 2004 to 2005, did you track the changing numbers of Americans at risk annually of dying prematurely because of excess poundage? You know it's a weighty issue when a $600,000–ad campaign challenges the CDC's original figure of 400,000 at-risk

Americans and that figure is then quickly reduced to 365,000—far too quickly for *any* rapid weight-loss diet. The Center for Consumer Freedom, funded largely by chain restaurants and food companies, attacked the CDC's numbers as "obesity myths." As of May 2005, the CDC had further lowered the number to 112,000 at-risk Americans. Who to believe? Do the numbers really matter anyway? Just look around. It's a fact: two out of three of us are fat, meaning overweight or obese. Surgeon General Carmona says obesity is a greater threat than terrorism. This condition diminishes our lives in more ways than shortening them. You would think the Center for Consumer Freedom was valiantly defending a constitutional guarantee implied in the pursuit of happiness: I can eat whatever I darn well want and in the quantities I want. It's my constitutional right to morph into a form resembling Jabba the Hutt. Tomorrow I'll follow the latest diet rage and instantly get the body of Angelina Jolie or Denzel Washington in svelte mode.

In part, the diet hype reflects the fact that nutrition is a very young science. Although Hippocrates said, "Let food be thy medicine," the strongest link between health and diet was first made by a Scottish naval surgeon who discovered in 1747 that citrus prevented scurvy. He knew the link was real, but he didn't know why. In 1905 William Fletcher connected beriberi to the eating of polished rice. (One wonders why it's taken another hundred years to leave the rice alone.) Our thirteen vitamins were discovered less than a century ago, and they weren't synthesized for another fifty years. We're the first generation to grow up with vitamin supplements. Not until 1992 was folic acid found to dramatically reduce the incidence of spina bifida births. In 1941 the Food and Nutrition Board of the National Academy of Sciences released the first Recommended Daily Allowances, including recommendations for calories and nine nutrients. In 1942 the "Basic Seven" food guide was released by the USDA; in 1956 the seven food groups were condensed to the "Basic Four"; and now we have six food groups with some very specific quantity restrictions. Who knows what will be on our plate in the future.

Adelle Davis was a pathfinder and became a nutritional guru when she published *Optimum Health* in 1935. She warned against eating too much sugar and noted that some diseases can be caused by a lack of certain foods. Her *Let's Eat Right to Stay Fit* (1954, 1970) was at the forefront of the whole-foods movement in California. Davis, by the way, earned a master's degree in biochemistry from the University of Southern California in the late 1930s. The study of food as a science originated with what used to be called home economics. In 1968 the University of Wisconsin–Madison formed a department of nutritional sciences. Dietetics became recognized as an academic study concurrent with the national passion for diet products. Hence the hundreds of diets since then. Now we spend $50 billion a year on weight loss and low-calorie foods and beverages. Yet 95 percent of people who pursue speed-diet remedies gain back all their weight within the time it took to lose it. Leading the bandwagon for the latest low-carb rage are the Scarsdale, Atkins, and Dr. Sears's "Enter the Zone" diets.

We boomers have to accept it: there is no miracle. There is no *rapid and sustainable* weight-loss diet. Moreover, there is no food that will set back our DNA, programmed to expire usually before we reach 120 years. It's the immutable truth: if you eat fewer calories than you burn, you'll lose weight. Another truth is that pork rinds in mass quantities aren't good for you. Yet we continue to ignore these truths and our common sense. The more outrageous, it seems, the more contagious. Remember when you and your girlfriends, hoping to lose ten pounds, went on the hardboiled egg and grapefruit diet three weeks before the 1967 homecoming?

It is significant to note that Adelle Davis died at age 70 of cancer; that Robert Atkins was hospitalized for cardiac arrest when he was 71 and died a year later from a head injury; that Herman Tarnower was murdered a year after he published his *Complete Scarsdale Medical Diet*. Given our track record (and that's the next topic here anyway), we'll jump at the next supermagical diet and spend millions on it. Before you buy into the next rage, though, Superwoman says, conquer the challenges standing between your first-adulthood body and your reengineered second-adulthood body.

## CHALLENGE
### If I Enjoy It, It Can't Be Exercise

Most of you boomer parents were able to hold weight gain at bay as long as you were playing with your kids. That's when exercise was fun because your little angels wanted you to race, skate, swim, hit, toss, or pitch with them. About the time they turned twelve, you noticed a shift in the dynamic. They got better, stronger, and faster than you. This was also the time when parents were supposed to adopt a nearly impossible tactic: deferring to your children's friends and teammates as their chosen playmates while staying involved in your kids' lives. You see, good parents become spectators. You provide transportation to playing fields, gyms, and studios, where you sit, watch, and cheer.

For Superwoman and her husband, this is when their own exercise became another item on the to-do list—to be squeezed in sometime before the morning commute or after washing the supper dishes and supervising homework. Exhaustion notwithstanding, you knew exercise would rev up the body for a sleepless night if you engaged in it three hours before bedtime. Besides, after the dinner and homework, you didn't *have* three hours before bedtime! So what did you do? You scheduled a daily run or exercise routine between 5:30 and 6:30 a.m.

Your husband bought into the hype that he could look like Rocky Balboa if he bought the right equipment. That's when the kids' playroom became the *family* fitness room (hubby did the sell on you). A pair of dumbbells and a mat, you said, were all you needed, and the living room is just fine. But he prevailed. It's that man-and-big-machine thing again. As long as it was state of the art, expensive, and conveniently "part of the family," your husband was sure he'd use it daily and start looking like a California governor in no time.

Wrong. Why? Because it wasn't fun. Then exercise became another appointment on the day's calendar when you joined a health club or hired a trainer. The unused exercise equipment became your trophies of guilt, of good intentions gone to flab (and to the billion-dollar exercise equipment industry). That's when the term *workout* became popular. The only way that we workaholic boomers could justify making time for exercise was to call it work. Work is something we schedule, make appointments for. It's a mandate for the day. It's also part of the human condition.

But the human condition is getting worse and worse because people don't exercise enough. We're told by all the MyPyramid, cancer, heart, and Alzheimer authorities that daily exercise is necessary to avert disease, as if body aesthetics weren't reason enough. We're still thinking, "Where, for heaven's sake, are we going to bleed out another hour from a day already suffering from time's tourniquet?" In short, we still equate exercise with work, not fun. And we know that in the long run, exercise has got to be fun, or at least enjoyable, to be sustainable. *Work?* We're retired now. We're supposed to be having *fun*. Aha, we're retired! Now we have ten hours of leisure time a day. Let the fun begin!

You've owned up to your first-adulthood boomer body obses-sions. Now you're ready to be all that you can be in your second adulthood. So, just do it! Do what? With all the conflicting and changing information, what is a boomer body to do? You need a plan—a sound plan without the hype. Again, Superwoman pres-ents a strategy from the reengineered workplace you just retired from.

## STRATEGY

### Initiate a Retirement Wellness Program

In 2005 General Motors spent more than $5.6 billion on health-care coverage for 1.1 million people. This coverage added $1,500 to the cost of every GM vehicle. The fact that this coverage was spent on 2.6 retirees per active employee reflects the beginning of a trend that economists say our retirement will only make worse.

Tens of millions of Americans are insured through their employers with low or no deductibles and no or low premiums. The year 2006 is the sixth consecutive year of double-digit increases in total corporate healthcare costs. Who pays? We all do. Through the price tags on our American-made consumer goods. To remain competitive in the global economy, these companies are reengineering their operations. One of these strategies involves putting more responsibility for health care on the employee through company wellness programs. Our country is doing the same. Whether it's our company or our country, we're in the swell of a major wave in human progress: the rethinking of health care from a treatment perspective to a prevention perspective. The money we save is the least of the rewards.

The concept of the company wellness program makes sense. It makes good sense because it encourages personal responsibility for one's health. Its goal is to engender lifestyle habits that help prevent the majority of chronic diseases. Recent research examining identical twins separated at birth indicates that only 20 to 30 percent of diseases are attributable to genes. That means that 70 to 80 percent of diseases are environmentally caused, most of which by *choices* we make. These choices include the quantity and quality of our nutrition and exercise. We'd much rather have Peter Jennings back than resurrect the Marlboro man, so snuffing out the butt should be a no-brainer by now. Sure, there are a lot of things out of our control that can go wrong with the human body, like the terrible autoimmune diseases, Parkinson's, and 30 percent of cancers. But here's a partial list of the diseases we can help control by lifestyle:

type II diabetes (blindness, kidney failure, amputation)

| | | |
|---|---|---|
| osteoarthritis | most cancers | stroke |
| sleep apnea | gallstones | gout |
| heart disease | liver disease | emphysema |

Smoking and having a body mass index over 25 are the choices most likely to do us out of a robust, complete second adulthood. Regardless of what anyone says, obesity is bad for you. The evidence of that is statistical and unassailable. That's the reason the steps and the climber were added to the 2005 MyPyramid.gov Web site, and it's the reason kids' body mass index is another element on their report cards. The United States spends more than $288 billion a year on weight-related health care. We can do better. We must do better. Given the knowledge, the tools, and the will to change, we *can* control the controllable. Because we carry so much weight in the body politic, our boom generation will set the example for the country to follow.

Retirement is the ideal time to change lifestyle habits because it's the beginning of a new life, our second adulthood. Habit changing is best accomplished when associative trigger stimuli are changed or eliminated. Our new daily environment and our choice of routine are ripe for change in every way. Superwoman, who has always had a more holistic view of life than her singularly career-focused husband, seizes the retirement opportunity to initiate a wellness program. She and her husband are about to change their me-generation to their re-generation by taking charge of their health. We can't change our chronological age, but we sure can change our feel, look, do, and interest ages. At the advent of a new century, let's be the generation to prove that we can be all that we can be—and haven't been yet. Set the pace and just do it!

Following is the wellness program this retired Superwoman and her husband have initiated for their marital partnership. It's based on the latest *medically credible* advice and common sense.

### Start with a Health-Screening Checklist

The Agency for Healthcare Research and Quality, part of the U.S. Department of Health and Human Services, has developed health-screening checklists for women and men accessible at www.ahrq.gov. These checklists include the most recent recommendations from the U.S. Preventive Services Task Force. They describe the health tests we need, when we need them, and why they are recommended. Additional sections address taking medicines to prevent disease, staying up-to-date with immunizations, and pursuing a healthy lifestyle. The idea here is for us to be informed so that we can be proactive with our health professionals in *preventing* disease. These checklists are appropriately titled "Stay Healthy at Any Age: Checklist for Your Next Checkup." There's one designed for men, and one for women. The healthcare consumer—that's us, folks—is charged with keeping track of when tests were last done and when they need to be done next.

A necessary sidebar here: This definitive source of healthcare information includes a screening test for depression. It says, "If you've felt 'down,' sad, or hopeless, and have felt little interest or pleasure in doing things for two weeks straight, talk to your doctor about whether he or she can screen you for depression." Depression is like any other illness. It has specific signs, symptoms, and treatments. According to the Center for Mental Health Services, clinical depression affects more than nineteen million American adults, as many as one in every thirty-three children, and one in eight adolescents. Although we're only in the nascent stages of exploring this new medical frontier, researchers have determined that depression can be the symptom of a chemical imbalance in the neurotransmitters, a biological condition that is treatable with medication. Depression can also be hereditary and can be triggered by stress, loss, or major lifestyle change. The latter is the reason that people transitioning into retirement need a heads-up.

## Know Your Family Tree

The hereditary element of some types of depression can also apply to other diseases. Whenever centenarians are interviewed, we all pay close attention to what they say when asked how they got there. Hoping to learn the "secret" of healthy longevity, we are told as many different secrets as there are centenarians (and some of those secrets, like eating a raw onion every morning, would be best kept to themselves and their constitutions). But there's one thing for certain: the centenarians have the genes, and they didn't do much in their hundred years to thwart them.

Thanks to Tony White's Celera project, the human genome was mapped in the year 2000. This monumental accomplishment is leading to the genetic analysis of our predisposition for certain diseases. Talk about a new frontier! This will be when medical intervention can head the bad guys off at the pass. Until then, we'll have to rely on what we know Mom and Granddad had and when they got it. But just because they had it, doesn't mean we will get it. Or just because they didn't, doesn't mean we won't. If your husband's father died of heart disease at age sixty-two, and his father died of the same disease at age fifty-eight, hubby sure enough better be vigilant about his cardiovascular health. Someday this guessing will sound so archaic, and that time is not far off. Thank you, Tony. Yours is more than one giant step for mankind.

### Eat to Live—Well

Doctors can make referrals to specialists, write prescriptions, and make lifestyle-change recommendations. But they can't see the specialist for us, they can't take the medication for us, and they certainly can't eat or exercise for us. After we have snuffed out the cigarettes, eating and exercising are the two lifestyle habits that can most profoundly influence our lives. A wellness program mandates that *we* take control.

When it comes to eating right, we have two concerns: nutrition and weight control. Nutrition is a concern. Period. Weight control is a concern when we are overweight or underweight. Believe it or not, not all of us are overweight, just 60 percent of us. *Just?* That's the *majority* of adult Americans! But you didn't get to be Superwoman by sitting back and accepting the status quo. To start the wellness program, Superwoman and her husband will compute where they are on the body mass index scale. Believe me, it's liberal. It's more forgiving than looking in the mirror or stepping on the scale and remembering how we used to look when we could just wear a smile and a Jantzen.

Body mass index is a more accurate measure than weight alone because it takes height into account. If we are highly muscular, à la Arnold Schwarzenegger or the Million Dollar Baby, the index will be skewed to the obese range. Otherwise, it's pretty accurate and a good indicator of whether we need to maintain, lose, or gain weight. It works like this:

| | BMI | Status |
|---|---|---|
| | Below 18.5 | Underweight |
| | 18.5–24.9 | Normal |
| | 25.0–29.9 | Overweight |
| | 30.0–39.9 | Obese |
| | 40 and above | Morbidly obese |

$$\frac{\text{weight in pounds}}{(\text{height in inches})^2} \times 703$$

If you're in the normal range, it means that your body is using up the calories you consume through normal metabolic functions and probably exercise. It means that your body is not storing leftover calories in fat cells. (Leftover calories are stored in 40 billion fat cells that can swell to six times their size and multiply to 100 billion.) The profile of your eating/exercising regimen in this normal range is diagramed as *calories ingested – calories burned = 0 calories stored.* If you're exercising 30 to 90 minutes per day and generally following the 2005 USDA recommended diet, then you can skip the rest of this section. You can go right on to the rest of your second-adulthood goals and be assured that you're working with your DNA potential to *have* second adulthoods. (Maybe you could offer yourselves as outside consultants for this wellness program.) Unfortunately, though, you are in the minority.

If you're in the underweight category, then you need to step up your nutritionally correct calories. Seek medical help if you're in the extreme of this category. Anorexia and bulimia are treatable diseases that afflict eleven million Americans. *Your* eating/exercise habits are diagramed as *calories ingested – calories burned = negative calories stored.* Exercise is still the component we cannot leave out of our balance between caloric intake and body weight because it is necessary in and of itself. When you are egregiously underweight, however, your body lacks the energy it needs from calories to maintain normal metabolic functions, let alone to sustain exercise. In this condition, the body consumes its muscle—like the heart—because there is no stored fat to draw from.

If you're in the overweight and above categories, you need to rally. Not rally in the sense of a crash diet (all those hypes that don't work anyway), but rally in the sense of setting a pace you can achieve, one that doesn't further add to your guilt every time you get on the scale, and one that is *sustainable*. As our children urge in other areas, get a life. Get a new lifestyle. We have the opportunity for one right here and now. So go for it!

Despite the diet industry trying its level best to convince us otherwise, weight control (unless you have a medically diagnosed problem) is a balance between calories eaten and calories used. If you're overweight, you are unbalanced. Your equation is *calories ingested – calories burned = surplus calories stored as fat*. The challenge in losing weight is shrinking these fat cells to the desired weight range. This is achieved through a *lifestyle* change of ingesting fewer calories and burning more through exercise. Once the desired weight is achieved, the maintenance level of *calories ingested – calories burned = 0 calories stored* can be enjoyed. Sounds easy? It really is, as long as we don't get impatient and expect a miracle tomorrow.

The MyPyramid.gov Web site is the tool Superwoman and her husband use for their wellness program's nutrition and weight-control component. It's the best available, and it's based on sound medical and nutritional advice. Because it's interactive, it customizes a daily plan according to one's age, gender, and physical activity. (It should, however, include height and bone structure.) For a sixty-year-old woman, for example, who engages in 30 to 60 minutes of physical activity daily, it recommends a 1,800-calorie-a-day plan with the following distribution from the six food groups:

| Grains | 6 ounces |
| Vegetables | 2.5 cups |
| Fruits | 1.5 cups |
| Milk | 3 cups |
| Meat & Beans | 5 ounces |
| Oils | 5 teaspoons |

You can get a feeling for how the calorie-eaten to calorie-burned ratio works when you enter "less than 30 minutes per day exercise." Then the total daily recommended calories become 1,600 (200 fewer); the recommended grains come down to 5 ounces; and the vegetables decrease to 2 cups.

These personalized plans have an added section titled "Discretionary Calories." This is my favorite section because it allows us to reward ourselves without guilt *if* we can balance the equation with the reward in it. It reminds me of my childhood confrontation with peas and carrots on my dinner plate, and my mother's words, "If you eat your vegetables, you can have dessert." If I promise MyPyramid.gov I'll exercise at least thirty minutes a day and eat the food-group quantities prescribed for my 1,800-calorie plan, I can eat 195 calories of something otherwise taboo.

Inside the Pyramid is a wealth of nutritional insight on the kinds of foods in each of the six groups, along with their calories. It gives sound guidance on maintaining body weight in the healthy range and preventing weight gain. It does not, however, customize a weight-loss diet for the user. (In our litigious society, this is a good decision. Besides, isn't it about time we start assuming responsibility for our own bodies?)

For overweight adults, MyPyramid recommends consulting a "healthcare provider about weight-loss strategies prior to starting a weight-reduction program to ensure appropriate management of other health conditions." And common sense dictates forgoing the discretionary calories treat. After the healthy target weight is achieved, and to sustain it, MyPyramid says, "About 60 minutes a day of moderate physical activity may be needed to prevent weight gain. For those who have lost weight, at least 60 to 90 minutes a day may be needed to maintain the weight loss. At the same time, calorie needs should not be exceeded." Your annual healthcare screening should detect any problems that will need monitoring while you are participating in this level of activity. If you're overweight, though (barring a medically diagnosed problem), one or both of these are probably true: you're too sedentary, and your diet doesn't bear much resemblance to the Pyramid.

This Superwoman's husband lost twelve pounds last year by walking vigorously 45 minutes most days of the week, by assuming some of the yard and housework formerly done by Superwoman, and by giving up cookies. How do you give up cookies? You just don't buy them. They no longer stare at us with their seductive chocolate chip eyes and say "eat me" when we open the cupboard. They are simply no longer an option in our new lifestyle of healthy eating. My hubby and I now keep a bag of minicarrots and a jar of no-salt toasted sunflower seeds in the refrigerator, and—this is a *miracle* for me—they've become my cookie substitute. I also grind golden flax and shake it with yeast flakes and skim milk for breakfast. My husband and I relish blueberries, strawberries, bananas, green tea, fresh spinach, raisins, nuts, and melons of every kind. We *never* drink sugared drinks. (In 2004 the average American drank thirty-seven gallons of sugared drinks—sixty thousand calories' worth!) We don't buy into the monster, ultimate, colossal, or enormous anything; we hold the mayo and salt; and we have exorcized French fries from our lives. We drink alcoholic beverages in moderation.

For most of us, simply giving up sweets and anything white in the grains group, holding down the bad fats, and limiting our portions will decrease calories. My husband and I made these habit changes to our diet after we computed our body mass indexes and studied what MyPyramid.gov recommended for us based on our ages and daily exercise levels. Initially, we used the Web site's MyPyramid Tracker Worksheet. We got the scoop on grains and carbohydrates by educating ourselves from the "tips" level of our customized Pyramid plan. Now we make a habit of examining the nutrition facts label (MyPyramid.gov has a section on that, too) or eating foods that don't need a nutrition facts label because they were made by Mother Nature. When our stepped-up exercise was added to these new lifestyle habits, we both lost weight in a sustainable way and gained a blush to our cheeks, a sparkle to our eyes, and tone to our regained muscle.

## Make Exercise Fun

Darwin told us that we're here today because we come from a long line of survivors. He called it the survival of the fittest. Just when we thought our brains assured our place at the top of the food chain, survival through physical fitness comes full circle. In our hunter-gatherer days, the strongest and the fittest got the meat and the berries. Now we drive to the grocery store, and everybody gets the hamburgers, chips, dip, ice cream, doughnuts, pie, and cookies to eat in front of three hours of television or the computer screen. The modern equivalent of hunting and gathering is doing us in. Sixty percent of us compromise our survival by a lack of fitness, a lifestyle choice we make.

The CDC says that 112,000 of us are being extinguished prematurely by excessive corpulence each year. And if we don't die from this body condition, we put ourselves at risk of living a diminished life with type II diabetes, hypertension, dyslipidemia, cardiovascular disease, stroke, gall bladder disease, respiratory dysfunction, gout, osteoarthritis, and certain kinds of cancers. Even

Alzheimer's disease has recently been added to this list. Doctors estimate that by 2020 fourteen million Americans could have Alzheimer's. An idle mind is the devil's workshop, and to a boomer, the devil's name is Alzheimer.

Research now says an idle mind means mental and physical inactivity. The brain needs good food, too. It uses up 20 percent of the energy of the entire body. So we need to feed it good stuff and keep its neurons firing by exercising it and the body that recharges it. Superwoman vows she will not let these lifestyle diseases destroy her or her husband's second adulthood. She doesn't want a trophy husband. She just wants to rejuvenate the one she's got . . . although Antonio Banderas or a body by Ralph Lauren would be . . . ah, forget it.

Her retirement wellness program, therefore, includes a fitness regimen of aerobic and weight-bearing exercises that are enjoyable and, therefore, sustainable. Again, she follows the Pyramid recommendations. To get her husband and her generation to endorse the reasons, she quotes the MyPyramid.gov section titled "Why is physical activity important?"

> Being physically active is a key element in living a longer, healthier, happier life. It can help relieve stress and can provide an overall feeling of well-being. Physical activity can also help you achieve and maintain a healthy weight and lower risk for chronic disease. The benefits of physical activity may include:
> Improves self-esteem and feelings of well-being
> Increases fitness level
> Helps build and maintain bones, muscles, and joints
> Builds endurance and muscle strength
> Enhances flexibility and posture
> Helps manage weight
> Lowers risk of [many chronic diseases]
> Reduces feelings of depression and anxiety

In short, exercise makes us feel better, look better, and live longer, and it adjusts our attitude. It is apparent that we all need to exercise for many reasons, besides the *necessity* it becomes when we're tipping the scales. In recognition of the epidemic that corpulence has become, the USDA added the climber and the stairs to the 2005 Food Pyramid, and Health and Human Services added chapters on "Weight Control" and on "Physical Activity" to its *Dietary Guidelines for Americans 2005*. Both organizations recommend aerobic exercise and weight training.

At a very minimum, *everyone* should be exercising 30 minutes a day in at least 10-minute bouts. To maintain body weight and avoid gradual weight gain (the average woman gains ten pounds a decade from age thirty), we need to exercise 60 minutes a day. To achieve weight loss, we need to participate in at least 60 to 90 minutes of moderate-intensity physical activity daily. All these activity levels, of course, assume that we not exceed our recommended caloric intake. These are aerobic recommendations that are fulfilled by activities that enhance our respiratory and circulatory systems, such as running, walking, swimming, dancing, and golfing sans cart. But the benefits of these activities (and others) are not limited to their aerobic benefits. They also build muscles where the target muscles are involved. But what about the other muscles? We have a body full of them. That's where resistance or weight-bearing exercises come in.

At age forty we start to lose a third of a pound of muscle annually and substitute it with fat (unless we decide we're going to compete with Father Time—and remember how boomers thrive on competition). When we select our weight-bearing exercises, we need to make sure that we target our whole body: our arms, shoulders, trunk, back, hips, and legs. These exercises need to be done every other day. Some say for 45-minute sessions; some say until at least eight to sixteen repetitions tire our muscles. A simple set of graduated hand weights works. Start with three- and five-pound weights, and then when eight-pounders are no longer a challenge, graduate to ten- or twelve-pound weights, and continue to work up from there. The point is always to challenge your muscles so they grow, or revitalize from fat. For every pound of muscle we build, our bodies burn an extra thirty-five to fifty calories a day. The MyPyramid.gov Web site details how much physical activity is needed. It also gives tips for increasing physical activity. Isn't it common sense, though, that playing wheelchair basketball or mowing the lawn with a push mower may be all the aerobic (or muscle-building) exercise you need for the day?

In case you need it, here's the rundown on exercise from *Dietary Guidelines 2005:*

| Moderate Physical Activity | Approximate Calories/Hr for a 154 lb Person |
|---|---|
| Hiking | 370 |
| Light gardening/yard work | 330 |
| Dancing | 330 |
| Golf (walking and carrying clubs) | 330 |
| Bicycling (<10 mph) | 290 |
| Walking (3.5 mph) | 280 |
| Weight lifting (general light workout) | 220 |
| Stretching | 180 |

| Vigorous Physical Activity | Approximate Calories/Hr for a 154 lb Person |
|---|---|
| Running/jogging (5 mph) | 590 |
| Bicycling (>10 mph) | 590 |
| Swimming (slow freestyle laps) | 510 |
| Aerobics | 480 |
| Walking (4.5 mph) | 460 |
| Heavy yard work (chopping wood) | 440 |

| Weight lifting (vigorous effort) | 440 |
| Basketball (vigorous) | 440 |

So, there you have it: use it or lose your opportunity to be all that you can be in second adulthood. The choice is yours. When all our government agencies are urging us to exercise 30 to 90 minutes a day to manage our weight, achieve weight loss, or maintain weight loss, we ask, "Now where am I going to find 90 minutes in my day?"

Stop! You're retired now. You've gained the ten hours a day that you used to give to work and the commute. Short of physical disability (and couldn't some of those wheelchair folks put our exercise routines to shame?), there are no excuses in retirement. *None.* You have the gift of time to accomplish what you want in your second adulthoods; exercise has to be a part of the plan if you want the rest. Maybe you can't rock around the clock, but you sure can twist again. This is when exercise moves out of the work category and becomes fun again. Let's "float like a butterfly and sting like a bee!"

If we don't want to do anything else, we can walk and make it fun by using it as our bonding time with friends or our spouse. And, thank goodness, walking is now chic! Almost all of us can "take a load off Fanny" by walking 60 to 90 minutes most days of the week. It requires only the skill of locomotion—not the kind we did to Little Eva's lyrics, but simply walking, the kind of motion that our feet were designed for.

Funny how exercise trends seem to follow boomer life stages. In our twenties and thirties tennis was de rigueur. We played spring and summer on teams—not for mere fun but for cut-throat competition in the guise of "it's just a game." The wintertime sport was skiing. We conquered moguls on black-diamond runs (at least that's how the après-ski stories went over a couple of glasses of wine).

Running in marathons (and training for them all year) coincided with our fourth decade on the fast track to yuppydom. We sported our trophy T-shirts that we just happened to be wearing almost all the time everywhere. Via these shirts we tacitly competed with our contemporaries in typical yuppy pecking order: (1) Paris Marathon, (2) New York Marathon, (3) Boston Marathon. When we weren't training or running in those marathons, we were playing handball or racquetball in the health clubs we gave rise to. Otherwise, we were skydiving or competing with Admiral Peary's feats at the North Pole or somebody's record somewhere.

By our fifth decade, running in 5- and 10-K charity events came into vogue. We flaunted the T-shirts that read, "I ran for the cure." At the same time, athleticism no longer had to pound the joints. Cycling in its various forms emerged as a must-do competitive sport: bicycling, mountain biking, motorcycling, dirt biking. This also was when the very expensive vacation sport of hang gliding or parasailing became popular—a must-do from Acapulco to the Alps.

By our mid-fifties, walking (we called it *power* walking), swimming, yoga, tai chi, and jazzercise had emerged. Now ballroom dancing is an exercise that's with-it, even for echo boomers! And—oh yes—golf, the rage. Just goes to show that our generation still holds the stopwatch.

So who's in charge of our health? Are we going to continue eating more than our daily allowance of poor calories? Are we going to continue spending our leisure time watching television or sitting at the computer? Are we going to continue believing the hype of the newest and latest body-rejuvenating miracle? And then, when we're suffering from one of the lifestyle-provoked chronic illnesses, are we going to expect our smarter-lifestyle-choice contemporaries and our offspring to *pay* for our choices?

Essential to our reengineered lives, nutrition and exercise are a way of sustaining our energy for second adulthood. That's it: exercise and nutrition provide a sustainable source of energy for twenty-first-century second adulthoods. We all know, for example, that clogged arteries create sticky wickets for blood flow to the heart, lungs, and brain. In our second adulthoods we have the opportunity to learn from our mistakes, undo them, and do things right this time. Unclog those arteries!

You're entering a healthcare milieu in which the "times they are a-changin'." A new application of Bob Dylan is appropriate. In his song, he implores senators and congressmen to support needed social change. They are doing so. In 2005 nearly 400 obesity-related bills were introduced in state legislatures, and a quarter of them were passed. Governor Mike Huckabee of Arkansas launched the Healthy Arkansas initiative to encourage his state's residents to quit smoking, exercise more, and eat better. As the head of the National Governors Association, he intends to implement the program nationwide. Likewise, former president Bill Clinton is spearheading the elimination of high-calorie, sugary drinks from school vending machines. This change will remove the equivalent of 1.5 pounds of sugar weekly from the diet of the average fifteen-to-nineteen-year-old. Huckabee and Clinton are both boomers, of course.

Thank goodness, too, that the House of Representatives voted 276–139 to bar consumers from suing the sellers of food they blame for obesity. When we silently defer to doctors for our health care and don't have a clue what prescription we're taking for what, do we have the right to sue them for negligence? Where is our responsibility for our own bodies? If we want to blame someone or something for our unfortunate bodies, we could always blame technology. Technology has removed exercise and sound nutrition from our daily lives. It has filled supermarket shelves with cheap,

mass-produced, good-tasting, calorie-laden food. It allows adver-
tisers to deliver incessant, irresponsible messages that say, "Eat or
drink this now" to find the fountain of youth. It affronts our intelligence with enticements that are oxymora: "All Natural
Sandwich: Meatless Chicken Salad" or "All Natural, No Fat, Low
Calorie Chocolate Mousse Cake." But who created this technology? Since when does a thinking person defer to technology anyway? Yes, advertising is consumer-driven, but we're not French
geese being force-fed and fattened for foie gras. We have the power
to change our consumer habits. It's called will power. Superwoman and her retired husband will lead the way. Our generation
and our civilization need to own up to the responsibility we have
to our own bodies. Start with Superwoman's wellness program.

## CHALLENGE
### I Refuse to Look My Age

"Mirror, mirror on the wall, who's the fairest of them all?" Yikes!
Is that me in that mirror? I don't look like that. Boomers used to
visualize themselves as they looked at sock hops when they were
falling in first love to Johnny Mathis's "Chances Are." Over the
years, though, these visual memories have morphed to more
updated self-images. In reality, I look more like Tara Banks, Eva
Mendes, or . . . Snow White—well, that's stretching it a bit—
maybe Sharon Stone. At least, that's what my memory tells me,
and I intend to get that mirror to concur. Who's in charge here,
anyway?

Yes, America is obsessed with beauty, and yes, Hollywood and
consumer marketing create the latest images of beauty. For
women—to date—beauty is the following:

- Any color skin, as long as it's wrinkle- and blemish-free
- A well-defined (only one) chin and neck

- A nose of any one of a number of descriptions, as long (but not too long) as it elegantly befits our ethnicity
- Voluptuous lips, which frame a full set of perfectly aligned, ultra-large, ultra-white teeth
- Eyes of any sparkling, gleaming color, set in defined sockets
- A muscle-toned, thin (except for D cups) body, hung on a well-proportioned skeleton

Ditto for men, minus the voluptuous lips and the pair of size D's but adding muscles by Bowflex and a skeleton at or above six feet.

Except for the skeleton (and medical science is working on that), all this is attainable, regardless of our natural endowments. Just another triumph of nurture over nature in the designer body of the third millennium. What healthy nutrition and rigorous exercise can't achieve, cosmetic procedures and cosmetic surgery can.

But America's beauty ideal is also linked to youth. Beyond a certain age, we're told, our youthful look succumbs to DNA programming. Fortunately, this doesn't apply to the forever-young boomer. That "certain age" is somewhere in the distant future, and DNA stands for we Do Not Age. To a great degree, boomers—male and female—just aren't buying that sappy, submissive stuff: "What counts is *inner* beauty," "True glamour is in your *attitude*," "It's all about aging *gracefully*." Instead, we paid $3.7 billion for 4.1 million cosmetic procedures in 2004, 44 percent of the country's total.

Superwoman aims to look like her feel, do, and interest ages, which have little to do with the number of candles on her birthday cake. Her husband, who is trying to convince *his* magic mirror on the wall that he really looks more like Will Smith or a six-foot Tom Cruise, feels the same.

## STRATEGY

### Tell That Mirror to Reflect the Inner Boomer

Workplace reengineering taught us to remake our professional selves to update the outmoded image of the corporation. Remaking the corporate persona included being downsized, outsourced, networked, delayered, empowered, TQM'd, one-minute managed, and customer-focused. In our career-controlled first adulthood, we adapted ourselves to a work environment that changed more often and more rapidly than any generation's work environment in history. Success was defined as being a part of the sea change, not simply staying afloat. The workplace changes we experienced over the past two decades were so dramatic that floaters eventually drowned.

Boomers accept change. Boomers were and still are change. Ever since Bob Dylan sang the overture to our era ("The Times They Are A-Changin'") boomers have thought making change was their anointed purpose. Now we are changing our lifestyle for a new life's epic we're still composing.

Superwoman, as leader in the boom generation's reengineering, uses this parallel as part of her strategy to accomplish Objective 6: Learn from First Adulthood (Morph That Body into a New Form). That is, get over whatever first adulthood has done to your appearance and, if you wish, update your image for second adulthood. Enough of us were replaced by technology in the workplace, so we certainly accept replacing what becomes nonfunctional. Some examples might include the following:

- Hip replacement
- Hair replacement
- Hair color replacement
- Hormone replacement

- Sex-drive replacement
- Digestive enzyme replacement

Some might even argue for spousal replacement, but Superwoman believes in reengineering, not replacing, husbands when they become nonfunctional. Christiaan Barnard performed the first heart replacement when we were in college. Replacement surgery became a way to renew life.

So why not youth replacement? You won't find many of the three million boomers who are already grandparents looking like Mr. and Mrs. Santa Claus. Nope, they're in their shorts or spandex and glowing from sit-ups, engagement with life, the joy of living in the skin they're in, or the magic of makeup and makeovers. It's our choice in this twenty-first century that is redefining age. If we choose, we don't have to look like whatever we imagine looking sixty to be. We know we can't end the thousand natural shocks that flesh is heir to; we just don't want to look like we've been through them all.

We've made nips, tucks, injections, lifts, and resurfacing one of the hot topics in pop culture. For many affluent boomers, if an $18,000 lift can give them a compromise between the face that launched a thousand ships and one that has borne the whips and scorns of time, they'll take it. One way or the other, if we're reengineering everything else about our lives, we might as well look like the re-generation. Besides, as L'Oreal taught us, we're worth it. We can always think of it as a long-term investment.

The number of cosmetic surgery and nonsurgical cosmetic procedures performed is increasing at the same rate that boomers turn forty. That's why it's said that these procedures have boomed over the past two decades. And these aesthetic improvements are not just for Hollywood and urban women anymore. Fifteen percent of them are performed on men. These procedures are elective, so insurance in most cases does not pay. To our generation, with an estimated annual spending power of more than $2 trillion, renewing youth through injection, scalpel, or laser is a good investment.

Please, don't ask Jennifer Aniston—*again*—what she thinks of Botox or cosmetic surgery! She's a Gen-Xer, born in 1969. Taking her advice is like taking Barbra Streisand seriously when she vowed to leave the country if President G. W. Bush was reelected. That was before she decided to stay and star in *Meet the Fockers*—not that this movie has anything to do with the subject at hand. But doesn't Dustin Hoffman's career personify the boomer journey? First, as Bernard in *Death of a Salesman*, then as Benjamin in *The Graduate*, Jack Crabb in *Little Big Man*, Carl Bernstein in *All the President's Men*, Ted in *Kramer vs. Kramer*, Michael Dorsey in *Tootsie*, Stanley Motss in *Wag the Dog*, and now Bernie in *Meet the Fockers*. Sorry—boomers do tend to digress about their generation's icons.

Let's face it. Superwoman and her husband learned the mantra from American culture and the workplace: image is everything. Their research reveals that the most common procedures are eyelid surgery, Botox injections, and liposuction. The Web sites of the American Society of Plastic Surgeons and the American Society for Aesthetic Plastic Surgery are reliable and informative places to become educated about board-certified plastic surgeons and the varieties of procedures. The latter site describes more than twenty procedures. If you choose to go this route, investigate thoroughly first.

"Mirror, mirror on the wall, who's the fairest of them all?"

Mirror answers: "I remember what you looked like at the end of your first adulthood. What's happened to you? You look great! You look like your inner boomer. Have you morphed into a regenerational form?"

## OBJECTIVE 7

# Move Out of Your Comfort Zone
### (Take Risks without Fear of Failure)

You're dead. Both of you. Your time's up. The eulogy read at your funeral is your résumé: degrees, jobs, positions, memberships . . .

## CHALLENGE
### My Life's Purpose Was My Job

By some power unknown to the living, you are each able to add to the eulogy: "This can't be all there was to my life. I had plans. I wasn't finished yet. I just never could . . . I was afraid that if I . . . I might fail. One thing led to another after I retired, and I slipped into a comfortable, quiet resignation with the way things were."

"C'mon," you say. "This is unfair. Why such a morbid vignette for two ready-to-go-get-'em boomers who've just been reengineered for their second adulthoods? Why go through all that training for a second adulthood if we're not going to have one? We have a vision for our future, we're transition survivors, we've practiced giving and getting love till we're practically perfect, and we've both thrown our chronological body clocks at the boob tube and doughnut shop. Now you want us to *die?*"

Calm down. This is just a simulation. You only role-play that you're dead. This is Superwoman's strategy for achieving Objective 7 in her reengineering of first adulthoods. If she and her husband are to move beyond the drop-into-apathy-and-let-the-world-go-by comfort zone of retirement, they need something to shake them up. Nothing like death.

By role-playing that your life ends with its first adulthood, you realize that there's got to be something beyond your job to define your life's purpose. With this wake-up call, you can steer your second adulthood into seizing the exciting new opportunities that allow you to be all that you can be—and haven't been yet. Most significantly, you can see the tragic waste of your unprecedented potential if you stay mired in boomer first-adulthood values that are self-limiting.

## STRATEGY
### Role-Play Out of Your Comfort Zone

So here's how this works. Superwoman will act first as administrator, and then she will become a participant along with her husband. As administrator, she describes the scenario, concurs with her husband on the desired outcome of the issue presented in the scenario, and finally provides preparation material that will inform their decisions in the role-playing. The rationale for choosing this strategy is its collaborative approach to reaching decisions and defining tasks in response to large changes.

Death is a large change. But remember the promise to your generation of living a *second* adulthood? You can't follow through on that promise without the death of first adulthood. In the role-playing, Superwoman and her husband together will represent two unified voices, one of first adulthood and one of second adulthood. The dead first adulthood (will be labeled *FA* in the upcoming challenge sections) makes its arguments from the long-held boomer point of view and offers three challenges to second adulthood (will be labeled *SA*). Second adulthood rebuts these challenges by describing opportunities to live a reevaluated life in the form of three imperatives:

- eradicating prejudice
- acquiring new knowledge
- assuming responsibility both for one's personal choices and for the obligations of American citizenship

In doing so, second adulthood accomplishes the desired outcome of the simulation, which is to empower Superwoman and her husband to move out of retirement's comfort zone and find the motivation to take the risks entailed in doing so, without fear of failure.

Superwoman as administrator provides the preparation, or stimulus, material necessary for focusing on the desired outcome. The first piece of preparatory material is the couple's retirement vision:

> We envision our retired lives to be an exciting second adulthood that presents unprecedented, limitless opportunities for our generation. We will positively adapt to change so that we can enjoy the challenges of the future, enrich our relationships, and appreciate our lives. We accept the obligations of discovering our unique gifts and of contributing positively to society. We will set the pace in redefining the human experience.

As Superwoman and her husband revisit the mission statement, they know to focus their role-playing on key concepts. They are reminded that the vision is a call to action. "Positively adapting to change" and "contributing positively to society" don't mean naval-gazing in an ashram.

Superwoman knows that she and her husband need a behavior-based approach to the role-playing that will define their second adulthoods' purpose. She also knows that *she* must initiate this call to action and steer her husband on the right path to second adulthood before he succumbs to the male, knee-jerk reaction—filling retirement's void with hair plugs, buying a Porsche, running after a cupcake, or retreating to that golf course for 8 of the 24/7.

Superwoman, therefore, consults *Man's Search for Ultimate Meaning,* in which Viktor Frankl explains his look-outside-ourselves philosophy for finding life's meaning. His is also a behavior-based model that we can use for our strategy. He says that by unselfishly serving a higher cause, we fully realize our humanity (or our second adulthoods, in this case). Frankl says that life asks of us its meaning (instead of the other way around), and we answer it in what we do, the way we choose to live our lives. "Self-transcendence," he argues, "is the essence of human existence." This transcendence happens when one is "actualizing himself . . . by giving himself . . . through serving a cause higher than himself or loving a person other than himself."

Frankl says that we must make a conscious effort to transcend our natural inclinations, which are by their nature selfish. Our success is measured in what we do for others. What does come naturally is habit (or all the challenges second-adulthood boomers face with their first-adulthood values). Frankl says each life situation we confront places a demand on us to act in a way that leads to self-actualization. This action comes from doing a deed or creating something, experiencing something or encountering someone, and changing ourselves by rising above and growing beyond ourselves when we face a fact that we cannot change. The fact none of us can change is the inevitability of our demise. The life situation we face is our opportunity to do something meaningful with our second adulthoods before this inevitability hits.

The strategy for meeting the objective before us (moving out of your comfort zone) is, you understand, sort of a combination of high Zen, or super-ecumenical thinking, and down-in-the-dirt corporate reengineering strategy. Why not? Role-playing is demonstratively (and you know because you've demonstrated on the job) an effective means for dealing with change. You did stuff like play the role of Pepsi when your company, Coca-Cola, was thinking of adding more sugar to "the Real Thing." Or maybe your exposure to this strategy was when you played the resuscitator of a dummy that had experienced a heart attack (which is a more appropriate analogy here). But role-playing worked. Its function here is for dead first adulthood (FA) to present challenges that must be addressed by second adulthood (SA) before second adulthood can begin its life truly unfettered.

Let the role-playing begin!

## CHALLENGE
### Beijing? Sure, as Long as I Can Stay in a Holiday Inn

FA: Come to think of it, I'd rather stay home because the outside world is dangerous and hostile.

SA: Now that you've got the time and flexibility to see the world, you're afraid? Fear is the most self-limiting of all human emotions. It's grounded in ignorance and prejudice. Prejudice is a mental and spiritual handicap that limits our capacity to grow to our human potential.

FA: What does prejudice have to do with my not wanting to visit a foreign culture?

SA: Would it surprise you that foreigners think Dallas is a city of opulent mega-mansions inhabited by oil billionaires who lead decadent lives? Would it surprise you that people of developing countries envision New York City as a lawless ghetto of warring gangs, gun-toting drug lords, and prostitutes? And conversely, Americans who have never visited Afghanistan ignorantly believe that all Afghans are fanatical Muslim nomads who live in caves. Travel is the best way to fight prejudices—ours and theirs.

FA: That goes both ways. They should come here if they think those things about our country.

SA: From those to whom much is given, much is expected. As American boomer retirees, you have the time and money to boldly go where no generation has gone before: Pekanbaru, Sumatra; Ouagadougou, Burkina Faso; Iquitos, Peru. You should go to developing countries because their people lack the opportunity and resources to come to you. In your vital second adulthoods, you should seek opportunities to walk outside the comfort zone that shelters your prejudices and feeds your ignorance. You're the first generation to retire in the global village. You have neighbors worldwide. Language doesn't have to be a barrier to mutual understanding when most communication is nonverbal anyway. Just by looking in their eyes and smiling, eating their food, and shaking their hands, you become ambassadors for world understanding.

FA: Ah, that's a big leap from the kind of vacation we took when we were raising kids. Back then, being the conscientious parents we were, we defined the "family vacation" as going where the kids' friends went—to the trails or the slopes or the beach or Disneyland. We agreed to go where their friends went, especially as they got older, in order to preserve the waning opportunities to bond with our children.

SA: Precisely! You were doing then what Viktor Frankl called acting according to the life situation confronting you. But that's the gift of your second adulthood: a new life situation to experience something new, leading to your growth. You've got time to go to the Uffizi and walk in the steps of St. Paul in Ephesus (those boring places your kids didn't want to visit), but you also should consider immersing yourself in a culture that allows you to step outside everything you consider comfortable. This is your second-adulthood opportunity for spiritual growth through encountering new people, as Frankl described.

If you really want cultural immersion, you could consider foreign volunteerism. There are abundant opportunities with groups such as the Peace Corps, International Executive Service Corps, WorldTeach, Doctors without Borders, Habitat for Humanity, and so on. Then you'd really be unselfishly serving a higher cause!

FA: But what if I just don't want to put up with all the hassle of bags, tickets, planes, time-zone changes?

SA: You don't have to go to a distant cranny of the planet to decrease prejudice and become an ambassador for world understanding. Prejudice is not limited to one country's ignorance of another. It could be our prejudice against people in our own city—just because we don't know them. The best way to get to know people you have a prejudice against is to work *with* them in doing something that improves your city, your country, the world. You know: think globally, act locally. We'll talk more about this when we address Objective 8, because volunteerism is classified as creativity, the next topic on the reengineering plan for second adulthoods.

FA: So you're saying I can take a local journey and still achieve the objective of getting out of my comfort zone?

SA: You betcha! Don't you remember what Mr. Rogers said for decades? "It's a beautiful day in this neighborhood, / A beautiful day for a neighbor." He was urging us and our children to go out and include our fellow city dwellers as our neighbors, in the highest sense of the term. Again, the rewards of this risk taking are many: You can take a journey that has an internal counterpart. You step out of time and routine. When you return, you're changed. You perceive life differently—with fresh sight, taste, smell, touch, and hearing . . . and fresh thinking. You've improved your global neighborhood.

Remember, too, that for centuries and across civilizations, an actual trip has been the way to launch a spiritual journey. You have just embarked: the world awaits you.

## CHALLENGE
### I Was a Recognized Expert in My Field. Why Do I Need More Education?

SA: Learning something new is one way to jump-start your second adulthood. To achieve goals you've never achieved before, you need to start *doing* things you've never done before. Acquiring new knowledge can be a goal in itself, or it can be the spark that ignites a latent passion. But you need to take the initiative to move out of your comfort zone of past-tense expertise.

FA: I don't get it. I acquired my education for my job. This education did what it was supposed to do: it put food on the table and it showed who's boss. What's wrong with that?

SA: Your paradigm—that's what's wrong with it. The cost-benefit approach was how you looked at education in your first adulthood. That's when your life was driven by the energy-devouring urgency to be successful and make money. You've been there, done that. In your second adulthood, you can learn any darn thing you want without worrying about whether it enhances your résumé.

FA: Well, actually, I enjoyed the synergy of the classroom, but that was so long ago. Colleges and universities are where you learn new stuff, and colleges and universities are only for kids—and maybe rising professionals spiffing up their curriculum vitae.

SA: Wrong, on two counts. Where have you been? Oh, I forgot. Consumed with your job. First, most colleges and universities also have lifelong-learning programs. Second, they're not the only continuing education venues that welcome folks like you. State public school systems offer courses, too. To locate them in your state, use a search engine such as Google to search for "continuing education courses" in your state. You can even take courses online from schools like MIT!

FA: What if I want to educate myself about something, but I don't want to be tied down to a timetable for learning it?

SA: You can buy audiotapes, videotapes, audio CDs, and DVDs of experts' lectures from places like The Teaching Company, for example, or you can borrow them from your public library.

FA: Well, I can't think of anything new I want to learn.

SA: Self-improvement doesn't come out of the air, and it certainly won't come with that attitude! As James Truslow Adams said, "There are obviously two educations. One should teach us how to make a living and the other how to live." It's time to learn for the intrinsic power it gives you and not simply for the dollar power. Just look at some of the catalogs and their course offerings—hard copy or online. How do some of these courses sound?

- Web Design
- Feng Shui
- Creating a Perennial Garden
- Astronomy: Touring Our Universe
- Latin Dancing
- The U.S. Supreme Court: An Abbreviated History
- Imperial Spain: Fact vs. Legend
- Lifetime Income Planning
- From Monet to Van Gogh: A History of Impressionism
- Great World Religions
- Chinese (or French, German, Japanese, Russian—any of a multitude of other languages)

Wow! There's so much out there just waiting for you to learn!

Another aspect of universities' lifelong-learning programs is that they offer educational travel programs that ensure that you have people-to-people contact with locals and have teachers as travel guides.

The new world that awaits you is anything beyond the boundaries of what you already know. The new world may be new skills, new knowledge, new physical challenges. The only failure you have to fear is stagnation, because that denies you a second adulthood.

## CHALLENGE
### It's Not My Fault—Therefore, It's Not My Problem

FA: Our generation gets blamed for the mess the country and the world are in. We can't help it that everything is going to hell in the hands of somebody else. We were born into the Age of Anxiety over nuclear annihilation, and we're retiring in the Age of Terrorism. We coped with the who-will-use-the-bomb-first angst by creating MAD, mutually assured destruction. In 1954 we even gave our fears a mascot, Alfred E. Neuman, and a slogan, "What, me worry?" But the threat of MAD doesn't work on an enemy yearning for apocalypse, on nihilists united only in their cult of death. What, me worry? I do. My fear pervades my thinking. This fearful thinking has created deep fissures in our country's civic psyche. I think we'll never put Humpty Dumpty together again. It's a gloomy world, one without much hope for the future. But it's not my problem.

SA: Don't you realize that your attitude is what our new arch-enemy hopes to achieve: erosion of our spiritual freedom and our optimism about creating a better world? Yes, this is categorically *our* problem and *our* responsibility. It's like what the courageous Bill Cosby says about responsibility for our choices, only on an international plane. The buck has passed to our generation. We need to be good citizens and leaders by example. At the very least, we can't resign ourselves to intimidation and negativity. My values determine who I am; our generation's values determine who we are. My values and what I do with them will be my greatest legacy.

FA: Well, then, just what should be second-adulthood values in these fearful times? This is a different situation than we faced with the Cold War.

SA: My values were voiced by William Faulkner in his 1950 Nobel Prize acceptance speech: man is immortal because he has a soul capable of "love and honor and pity and pride and compassion and sacrifice." I believe in the transcendence of the human spirit. At this stage in my life, I feel I have the courage to ask, *Am I what I can't believe in?* I am, moreover, willing to take the risks to craft a better world—without the fear that inhibited me earlier. After all, it's my legacy we're talking about. And I now have the wisdom, time, and responsibility to make the world a better place by starting right here at home.

FA: Besides being called the me-generation, we've earned the reputation for being the no-fault generation. A reputation is a tough thing to live down. Blaming others for our problems and seeing ourselves as victims have led to the anti-ethic of "Don't blame me. It's not my fault." In the early 1970s we used the defense "I was only following orders" or "It's not a crime until I get caught, and then I can always blame poor litigation if I can't convince a jury that I was a victim. Besides, everybody else does it." From Watergate to Abu Ghraib, that's how we think.

Remember how David Berkowitz, the "Son of Sam," claimed a dog told him to murder six people in 1977? Remember how the attorneys for Dan White, who murdered San Francisco's mayor and city supervisor in 1978, argued that White was the victim of junk food? Remember how the subliminal messages in a Judas Priest recording were blamed for a double suicide in 1985? Remember when the MTV show *Jackass* was blamed in 2001 for a 13-year-old being set afire by friends? For the 9/11 intelligence failures, Republicans blamed Bill Clinton, Democrats blamed George W. Bush, the FBI blamed the CIA, and the CIA blamed the FBI. Speaking of blame, category-five-force blame whirled in all directions around Hurricane Katrina's devastation of New Orleans.

SA: Liability is useful and good when reasonable and warranted, but people use it in place of personal responsibility. What we need to work on is personal responsibility.

FA: It's as if we're using fear and intimidation as a weapon of mass self-destruction. In *The Collapse of the Common Good* Philip Howard said the idea of a legal threat has undermined our freedom by making us fearful: "Americans no longer feel free to do what we believe is right. Ordinary choices are burdened with legal fear and argument. Cooperation of all kinds has become risky. Daily interactions are imbued with distrust. Is the doctor free to act on his best judgment? Does the teacher have the authority to run the classroom?"

But it's not my fault that juries awarded $640,000 to Stella Liebeck, who sued McDonald's for selling her coffee that burned her when she spilled it in her lap; or $9,900,000 to a New York City woman who sued the city for injuries she incurred when she lay across subway tracks in a suicide attempt. It's not my fault that families filed a $5 billion lawsuit against videogame companies for the thirteen murders committed by Dylan Klebold and Eric Harris at Columbine High School in 1999. Nor is it my fault that Medicare formally recognized obesity as an illness in July 2004, which will result in billions of American tax dollars paying for weight-loss programs and stomach stapling. So, put that in your pipe and smoke it—and hey, then you can sue the tobacco companies!

SA: Within the last half decade, signs of personal responsibility have been emerging. The Personal Responsibility in Food Consumption Act, known as the Cheeseburger Bill, was passed by the House in 2004. It dismisses civil actions that seek to sue the fast-food industry for the diet-related health problems of individuals who choose to gorge themselves on this food. Call it bottom-line accountability.

Another sign is the new accountability posture against twenty-first-century robber barons. In the 1980s prosecutors extracted large financial settlements from firms whose executives were guilty of malfeasance. The executives themselves were not prosecuted; hence they were left in place to exploit again. Within the past several years, local and federal prosecutors have started pursuing individuals rather than the companies that employ them. No longer are these corporate heads illegally making the megabucks and passing the blame. Now a host of former CEOs and CFOs are facing up to their no-fault posture in prison. Be careful what you live for.

A whole pack of CEO and CFO wolves in pinstriped suits defended their rapacious greed with you've-got-to-be-kidding excuses like ignorance of the company's accounting, committing fraud to save the company, denying responsibility for theft because of being CEO in name only, acquiring an irresponsibility image created by the media. Their stories have been as unbelievable as a reality show—except for the thousands who lost their jobs, company stock, and retirement savings. But thanks to the Sarbanes-Oxley Act of 2002, which says chief executives must now personally sign off on financial statements, and prosecutors who are going after the chiefs, not their tents, we are entering a new era of corporate responsibility.

FA: Our society encourages greed. Look at the outrageous payouts and pensions given by boards to top executives when they leave their companies: $113 million to Philip Purcell of Morgan Stanley in June 2005; $32 million to Stephen Crawford, copresident of Morgan Stanley, in July 2005; $600,000 per year to Harry Stonecipher of Boeing in March 2005; $21 million to Carly Fiorina of Hewlett-Packard in February 2005; and $1.4 million per year to Franklin Raines of Fannie Mae in December 2004.

SA: Our society encourages greed, you say? Who is "our society"? *We* are "our society." Are you just going to complain? If you're a shareholder in any of these companies, you have recourse. Boards of directors make these decisions. They should be held accountable. Write to the companies. Write to your congressmen.

Get involved. Become an informed citizen. If information is out there, you can retrieve it instantly through the Internet, and you can be heard through e-mail and blogs. We live in a wonderfully transparent world, but we need to use these tools to be participatory citizens.

FA: I feel powerless; that's why I don't vote. Besides, I was always too busy to get to the polls.

SA: Any American who doesn't vote doesn't deserve to be an American. Any American who complains about the status quo and doesn't vote is a hypocrite. Did you know that 63,042,191 Americans voted in the 2004 presidential election? That was approximately 30 percent of eligible voters. And a much lower percentage of Americans vote in their local elections. To illustrate where our values lie, sixty-five million votes were cast for an American Idol in 2004. Jury duty, another privilege given us as beneficiaries of the Magna Carta, is considered by too many of us to be an inconvenience, an intrusion, and a hardship.

F.A.: Okay, so what can I do about changing my rap, or my rep, as the no-fault generation? How can you improve personal responsibility?

S.A.: You can start first by being the change you wish to see in the world, as Mahatma Gandhi said. Exercise your obligations— really your privileges—as a citizen by voting and serving on jury duty. After this, encourage others, especially your children and their children. (There are Web sites already in place that you can visit, or you can start conscience-arousing programs of your own.) To assume that *things just happen to us* is impotent and inept and all the things that our generation does *not* believe in. We must light the fire for future generations, or at least reignite it if we've bought into the lazy excuse or deferential-impotence argument of "those others who have the power." We have the power. We have the power *more than ever* in retirement.

We have the time, the accumulated wisdom, and the expertise. If we waste it, we will tacitly tell our children and their children that democracy is a spectator sport. Our legacy will be the demise of our representative government. But we can't—we won't—allow this to happen! Let us be the generation that re-instills personal responsibility into the collective American DNA. Let's stop booming about how we're victims. We can talk, argue, complain, debate, and polarize to our graves, but it's time we do something about our generation's mind-set about victimhood. At the very least, we should vote and be jurors and educate the succeeding generations about the importance of a participatory citizenship. Surely boomers still have some faint desire for proactive involvement smoldering in their psyches. Rekindle it!

## OBJECTIVE 8

### Find Your Giftedness

(The Joy—and Your Legacy—Follows)

"I can't get no satisfaction . . . I try and I try and I try and I try . . . " Thus the Rolling Stones gave voice to the boom generation's animus. That was 1965. The Stones (at least what's left of them) are still singing it in 2006—to the same boomers still looking for satisfaction. We've certainly tried. We've accumulated more wealth, education, power, and things than any generation in history. But we're still not satisfied. Our generation created the cultural imperatives that size matters and more is better, so how can we ever see our lives as a glass half full when we keep making the glass bigger?

Maybe we need to rethink what we're putting in the glass. In 1964, the year of our emancipation, we made the automobile our generation's status symbol in three top-of-the-chart songs, the Beach Boys' "Fun, Fun, Fun," the Rip Chords' "Hey, Little Cobra," and Ronnie and the Daytonas' "GTO." These pop songs identified our generation's emerging values with the speed, freedom, and material status of driving and owning the T-Bird, Cadillac, Stingray, XKE, Jag, and GTO. Now our love affair with the car has become our marriage to the automobile. Its gas tank is like our life's drinking glass—we keep putting more in it only to find we're running on empty a week later.

Our generation is poised at the starting block of a new era in human history. We are the first generation to have before us what only the highly privileged have enjoyed in the past: the security to "retire" into decades of leisure time. We are looking at an entire second adulthood of leisure time, and an opportunity to measure our self-worth by something other than our net worth—an opportunity to fill life's glass with satisfaction. But how?

Superwoman knows. Superwoman knows because the "how" has always been there. It's something she put aside or redirected while child raising, homemaking, multitasking, and barrier breaking. It's a passion to express her uniqueness, to create something out of her spirit, to craft something compelling out of her destiny. She knows now is the time to awaken that smoldering passion. Her husband, however, is still looking backward. He thinks, "Yesterday was the time."

## CHALLENGE
### I'm Not Creative and Besides, I've Made My Life's Contribution

Is Superwoman going to let her hubby lie back and watch his mojo expire? Not on her life—certainly not on the promise for their new lives. Their partnership marriage is a collaborative endeavor. Superwoman won't let her husband roll over and play finished when they're just temporarily out of sync. This is their opportunity to put the icing on retirement's cake, or rather to be the leading edge of a generation that can have its cake and create another one, too. She just has to do a little more reengineering of the outmoded first-adulthood thinking that his life's contribution was his job and all the stuff that salaries buy.

That thinking is why retirement got the reputation of being the end of productivity and contribution, of being the pasture people are put out to, albeit with eighteen holes and flags. As the first generation of twenty-first-century retirees, the arena is now ours. We don't intend to be spectators. Regardless of how we felt about our first adulthoods' wage-earning jobs, now we can pursue our passions without the fear of risk taking that inhibited us earlier. Given the human desire to make a mark on the world, to leave a footprint for others to follow, and given our extended health and accumulated wisdom, we are the generation to redefine the human experience.

But first, Superwoman must help her husband *realize* the potential in his second adulthood. She knows that a whole new life of exciting opportunities awaits them both. Now, as never before in their lives, she and her husband have the opportunity to manifest the innate creative potentials that lie within them, to find the sublime part of their humanity.

## STRATEGY
### Find Your Latent Creativity

It's tempting for Superwoman to succumb to her dark side and say, "Creative? Not *my* tunnel-visioned husband!" and then to let him carve his life's purpose from his par, while she achieves her eternity by contributing her unique gift to the world. Tempting . . . but, nah, the whole idea here is for Superwoman to lead the way for the seventy-seven million of her generation and all the generations to follow. If boomers are to raise the level of the game of life, we have to be the generation on first base, and for "coach" Superwoman this means putting her husband up to bat.

Again, she gets her game plan from the reengineering strategy they're both familiar with. She explains that their first adulthood was analogous to the business-as-usual mode that developed in America after World War II. That mode was abruptly outmoded by technology and the global marketplace in the last decades of the twentieth century. The Superwoman-husband team's second adulthood is analogous to the new business environment that gave rise to reengineering in those decades. There was no precedent for the new situation. To stay competitive—even viable—businesses had to come up with new ideas and fresh approaches. Status quo was out. Creativity was in. Likewise, there is no precedent in human history for our second adulthood. To remain productive— even vital—boomers must come up with new ideas and fresh approaches to life. The status quo of first adulthood is out. Creativity is the key.

The Superwoman-husband team is again guided by their retirement vision, the part that says, "We accept the obligations of discovering our unique gifts and of contributing positively to society." They determine that Objective 8, Find Your Giftedness (The Joy—and Your Legacy—Follows), will fulfill this part of their vision for second adulthood. Superwoman, as manager-leader of the team, knows she has to foster her husband's participation and share information that contributes to the accomplishment of this objective. Together they assess the issues inherent in the challenge—the boomer male thinking that he is not creative and that his first adulthood's job was his contribution to life.

Superwoman's strategic approach looks like a variation on the cosmic questions, but then, why not, when we're talking about the quintessence of a new life? The strategic plan to find and manifest creative potential answers these questions:

- Why should I?
- What is it?
- Where is mine?
- How do I use it?

### Why Should I?

Superwoman addresses the question of *why* in the form of a situation assessment. The situation is this: You have a choice. If you choose not to pursue your creative potential, you're denying yourself—and others—your unique gift. You're denying your opportunity to be fully human, to do what the seers and prophets (and Superwoman) believe we were put on this planet to do. You are resigning yourself to a *continuation* adulthood of trying to find satisfaction, most likely in the same way you couldn't find it the first time—by being a serial spender. You'll always be looking backward, wanting to "get your groove back." You'll be looking for this lost groove in sand traps, second homes, and the latest model SUV. You'll think of your good fortune as a birthright—or worse, entitlement—instead of treating it as a debt that has to be repaid. You will be denying that there is a need beyond the confines of self.

However, you can instead accept the good fortune of having a second adulthood as an opportunity to unleash your potential for personal growth and self-expression. You can find within you what gives you joy, not simply satisfaction. In doing so, you will contribute to the lives of others and be an example of how the really good life is lived for future generations. You'll redeem your generation from its me-generation label by becoming the re-generation.

After this assessment of the situation, surely Superwoman's husband will come clean and admit that he wants more from his new life than an arcadia of daily tee times. So, before that little man jumps out of the TV screen and asks, "What's in *your* ethical will?" you'd better do something besides look in your wallet.

### What Is It?

To our generation, so driven by materialism, creativity is the arcane ability to paint, compose music, or write a novel. It's something possessed only by weird impoverished geniuses (think *Amadeus,* the movie) or by creatives who live physically and psychically blemished lives (think Van Gogh without his ear, and Toulouse-Lautrec in John Huston's 1952 *Moulin Rouge*) or by artists who could pursue their obsessive genius (think Michelangelo) because they had equally obsessive patrons on unlimited bank accounts (think Pope Julius II, the Medici) who wanted to be immortalized. To boomer men, creativity is either frippery or something done by outer-fringe boomers who never got over turning on, tuning in, and dropping out (the ones who went to Haight-Ashbury, lived on marijuana-growing communes, and permanently dropped out of the mainstream and missed the boomer awakening of shopping-center development and going for the buck on Wall Street). Worthwhile creativity, he thinks, is how his intuition made a dollar from a dime.

Obviously, Superwoman needs to instill a more enlightened definition. Her task here is to dispel negative stereotypes and misconceptions about the nature of creativity. Boomers have a limited idea of giftedness because when we were coming along there was only Stanford-Binet verbal and math. We thought we were smart—or even "gifted"—if we knew square roots and could read Shakespeare. In 1983 Harvard education professor Howard Gardner changed that narrow (very post–World War II academic) way of looking at giftedness. He said we humans have multiple intelligences, and at that time he identified seven: mathematical, verbal, spatial, kinesthetic, musical, interpersonal, and intrapersonal. In 1993 Thomas Armstrong popularized Gardner's theory in *7 Kinds of Smart: Identifying and Developing Your Multiple Intelligences.* Gardner subsequently added "naturalist" as an eighth intelligence. The multiple-intelligence theory broadened education's definition of giftedness. The idea now is that everybody is gifted; it's just a matter of finding your particular gifts.

### Where Is Mine?

So, before Superwoman's husband can come up with change-resistant, specious excuses like "My dog ate my talent" or "I can't do that; I've never done it before," she uses Armstrong's explanation of the first seven categories of intelligence and Gardner's added definition of naturalist intelligence to help her husband detect where his untapped creativity may lie.

The first kind of smart, *linguistic intelligence,* is the intelligence of *words.* This is the intelligence of the journalist, storyteller, poet, and lawyer. It's the kind of thinking that brought us Shakespeare's *King Lear,* Homer's *Odyssey,* and the tales of the Arabian nights. People who are particularly smart in this area can argue, persuade, entertain, or instruct effectively through the spoken word. They often love to play around with the sounds of language through puns, word games, and tongue twisters. Sometimes they're also trivia experts because of their ability to retain facts in their mind. Or alternatively, they're masters of literacy. They read voraciously, can write clearly, and can gain meaning in other ways from the medium of print.

The second kind of smart, *logical-mathematical,* is the intelligence of *numbers* and *logic.* This is the intelligence of the scientist, accountant, and computer programmer. Newton tapped into it when he invented the calculus. So did Einstein when he developed his theory of relativity. Traits of a logical-mathematically–inclined individual include the ability to reason, sequence, think in terms of cause-and-effect, create hypotheses, look for conceptual regularities or numerical patterns, and enjoy a generally rational outlook on life.

*Spatial* intelligence is the third kind of smart and involves thinking in *pictures* and *images* and the ability to perceive, transform, and re-create different aspects of the visual-spatial world. As such it's the playground of architects, photographers, artists, pilots, and mechanical engineers. Whoever designed the Pyramids in Egypt had a lot of this intelligence. So too did individuals like Thomas Edison, Pablo Picasso, and Ansel Adams. High spatial individuals often have an acute sensitivity to visual details and can visualize vividly, draw or sketch their ideas graphically, and orient themselves in three-dimensional space with ease.

*Musical* intelligence is the fourth kind of smart. Key features of this intelligence are the capacity to perceive, appreciate, and produce rhythms and melodies. It's the intelligence of a Bach, Beethoven, or Brahms, and also that of a Balinese gamelan player or a Yugoslavian epic singer. Yet musical intelligence also resides in the mind of any individual who has a good ear, can sing in tune, keep time to music, and listen to different musical selections with some degree of discernment.

The fifth intelligence, *bodily-kinesthetic,* is the intelligence of the *physical* self. It includes talent in controlling one's body movements and also in handling objects skillfully. Athletes, craftspeople, mechanics, and surgeons possess a great measure of this kind of thinking. So too did Charlie Chaplin, who drew upon it in order to perform his many ingenious routines as the "Little Tramp." Body-smart individuals can be skilled at sewing, carpentry, or model-building. Or they may enjoy physical pursuits like hiking, dancing, jogging, camping, swimming, or boating. They're hands-on people who have good tactile sensitivity, need to move their bodies frequently, and get "gut reactions" to things.

The sixth intelligence is *interpersonal.* This is the ability to understand and work with other people. In particular, it requires a capacity to perceive and be responsive to the moods, temperaments, intentions, and desires of others. A social director on a cruise ship needs to have this intelligence. So does an administrator of a large corporation. An interpersonally intelligent individual may be very compassionate and socially responsible like Mahatma Gandhi, or manipulative and cunning like Machiavelli. But they all have the ability to get inside the skin of another person and view the world from that individual's perspective. As such they make wonderful networkers, negotiators, and teachers.

The final [seventh] intelligence is *intrapersonal* or the intelligence of the inner self. A person strong in this kind of smart can easily access her own feelings, discriminate between many different kinds of inner emotional states, and use her self-understanding to enrich and guide her life. Examples of individuals intelligent in this way include counselors, theologians, and self-employed businesspeople. They can be very introspective and enjoy meditation, contemplation, or other forms of deep soul-searching. On the other hand they might be fiercely independent, highly goal-directed, and intensely self-disciplined. But in any case they're in a class by themselves and prefer to work on their own rather than with others.

Gardner's eighth intelligence is *naturalist.* He describes this intelligence as the ability to discriminate among living things in the plant and animal kingdoms. Furthermore, the naturalist has the ability to discern order and pattern and to make distinctions that define difference. Gardner says this intelligence is used by the botanist, the chef, and the discerning consumer. Those gifted with this intelligence include Galileo, Rachael Carson, John Audubon, Lewis & Clark, Jane Goodall, Jacques Costeau, Diana Fossey, John Muir, and Sacajawea.

Gardner says we all have these intelligences to one degree or another. But there's one that will beckon you if you'll examine what you love doing.

- Listen to the voice within you.
- Keep an open mind.
- Go on a vacation or a wilderness journey. Physically get away from routine.
- Ask your friends and family what they think you're good at.
- Fill in the blank: "If I had my life to live over again, I would ___."

Imagine! You *do* have another life, with the bonus of not having to be a teenager again, not having to *raise* a teenager again, and not having to earn a living.

This freedom from first-adulthood responsibilities is also called leisure time. This leisure time is yet another factor that contributes to the realization of latent creativity. History teaches us that self-chosen creative activity is possible only when one is freed from workaday obligations, or when one is fortunate enough to make a living from one's creativity. Two hundred years ago, Wordsworth lamented, "Getting and spending we lay waste our powers." Thoreau protested the mid-nineteenth-century acquisitiveness that denied what he called "true wealth," sufficient leisure for creativity. Thoreau went off to his one-room cabin for two years to live a life of simplicity and write about it. He said in his journal later published as *Walden*, "I left the woods for as good a reason as I went there. Perhaps it seemed to me that I had several more lives to live, and could not spare any more time for that one." Thoreau died fifteen years later, at age forty-four. Just imagine what he could have done with a second adulthood of his own! So another standard excuse for not pursuing one's giftedness ("there's no time") is shot down. Neither can Superwoman's husband argue that manifesting his creativity requires the planetary alignment of talent with the right place and time. There has never been a place (these United States) more conducive to and accepting of innovation, nor has humanity ever had so much time to be creative. Our second adulthood gives us the time and place to examine potentials that we eclipsed in our first adulthood.

There's another bonus—a great one! Gene Cohen, an expert in tapping creative potential in the second half of life, says our interpersonal and intrapersonal intelligences grow with time and experience. Makes sense! The longer we live, the more we develop social and emotional understanding of ourselves and others. This means we have, just by being in our second adulthood, a greater giftedness in the personal intelligences than our Gen-X or millennial offspring! To be creative, then, means doing something new using one of our eight intelligences.

### How Do I Use It?

The corporate world you and your husband just left now recognizes the importance of the personal intelligences, collectively called "emotional intelligence" by Daniel Goleman. Indeed, Goleman asserts that emotional intelligence can matter more than IQ in achieving success. Leaders gotta have it. So do lasting marriages, as Superwoman showed in the discussion of Objective 3, Listen with Heart (What Partners Want). This gift of empathy and sensitivity and knowing how to listen and respond with heart is rare in the young. Because our experiences with life have ripened our interpersonal and intrapersonal intelligences into giftedness, we as a generation are qualified for social service and caring activities.

Making the choice to find and use your giftedness is not only self-rewarding; it also contributes to the lives of others. Viktor

Frankl guided us in moving out of our comfort zones through what we do. Here again, we answer what life asks of us by *using* our gifts. We are also defining the sublime within us. There are two ways we can use these gifts. Gene Cohen says our creativity in its eight forms can be manifested publicly or privately. He points out, moreover, that everyone has public or private (maybe both) creative potential ready to blossom in at least one of the intelligences.

Contributions recognized by others represent public creativity. The contributions of eight Americans of our time—Langston Hughes, Martin Luther King Jr., Bernie and Billi Marcus, Ted Turner, Oprah Winfrey, and Bill and Melinda Gates—can be used to represent public creativity in various combinations of the eight forms of giftedness. For example:

Langston Hughes's "Theme for English B" exemplifies linguistic, interpersonal, and intrapersonal gifts coming together in one supremely eloquent, forty-one-line poem. His contemporary, Martin Luther King Jr., possessed the same gifts, along with musical intelligence. King used his gifts to contribute to the civil rights movement, a legacy that defines what it means to be American. In 1964 King won the Nobel Peace Prize. All four of his gifts manifested publicly are apparent in the content and musical cadence of his famous "I Have a Dream" speech. Hughes died one year before King. Their legacies live and continue to inspire enlightenment.

Bernie Marcus, cofounder of Home Depot, and his wife, Billi, embody interpersonal and intrapersonal gifts in ways that drive their desire to help others realize their gifts. Their Marcus Institute helps children with acute developmental disabilities turn their disabilities into possibilities. In addition, they gave $200 million to help establish the world's largest aquarium, a centerpiece for the city of Atlanta's second resurgence and an aquatic eco-laboratory without parallel. Bernie and Billi Marcus say the Marcus Institute and the Georgia Aquarium are their gifts to Atlanta and Georgia. It can be said as well that the Institute and Aquarium are the Marcuses' own gifts of interpersonal and intrapersonal intelligence made manifest.

Ted Turner represents the confluence of bodily kinesthetic, spatial, linguistic, naturalist, and personal intelligences. Witness his visionary creation of global and bilingual news networks, the international sports Goodwill Games, his film and film-restoration library, youth development programs in rural communities, the United Nations Foundation, and the Nuclear Threat Initiative. Ted Turner also founded the Turner Foundation, which supports water, air, wildlife, ecology, and recycling initiatives. The Ted Turner Endangered Species Fund works to conserve biodiversity.

Oprah Winfrey may be today's paramount example of being the change you wish to see in the world. She is messianic in sharing her linguistic, spatial, and personal intelligence gifts. Her mega-media career reflects her vision for inspiring goodness and the development of human potential. As a philanthropist, she founded the Oprah Winfrey Foundation, which targets women and children through education and empowerment programs. Through Oprah's Angel Network, she encourages others to experience the joy of giving. In 1991 she initiated the National Child Protection Act. In 2002 she visited South African orphanages and personally gave toys, clothes, food, books, and school supplies to fifty thousand children. Her Oprah Winfrey Leadership Academy for Girls opens in South Africa in 2007. *Time* magazine has repeatedly named Oprah Winfrey among the hundred most influential people of the twentieth century. She has received a prodigious list of prestigious awards. But often just her smile says it all. It certainly speaks to the thousands who draw daily inspiration from her.

Bill Gates has used his exceptional logical, mathematical gift to make computers the tools they are today. Not only is he chairman and chief software architect of Microsoft Corporation, he has authored two books that show how computer technology can solve business problems and determine the future. Through the Bill and Melinda Gates Foundation, he and his wife have used their intrapersonal and interpersonal gifts on a global scale by committing $27 billion to health and learning. They embrace the idea that empowering others through education and behavior change is essential to fighting AIDS. They are committed to the eradication of malaria, which killed four million babies in 2005. Some wonder whether Bill Gates derives more pleasure from his work or from his philanthropy, both of which reflect his tremendous creativity.

Although you and your husband may never be indexed in a history book, you now have the opportunity to contribute something valuable to your community, your culture, and—who knows—the world. Within one of your multiple intelligences resides an idea, a spark that is waiting to be ignited. There are myriad opportunities—and societal needs—for your public creativity. Community service, or volunteerism, is one way you can be publicly creative.

The inspiration of John F. Kennedy's call to citizenship resounds in the baby boomer memory: "And so, my fellow Americans, ask not what your country can do for you; ask what you can do for your country." And so we did. We established the Peace Corps, we supported civil rights legislation, we began the human rights movement, and we opened our eyes to the damage caused by pollution and to the fragile eco-balance of our planet.

But during the 1970s our generation moved from this sense of obligation to community to a looking-out-for-number-one mentality. As a consequence, baby boomers were labeled the *me-generation*. In the 1980s we acquired the go-get-your-piece-of-the-pie-and-to-hell-with-everybody-else label. The stock market highs and unemployment lows of the 1990s confirmed our conviction: hard work pays off. We enjoyed the rewards; nothing else really mattered. Most boomers were too concerned with acquiring more status symbols to care much about their community, much less the country's or the world's problems. Granted, the world was rather calm, relatively speaking, and the United States was enjoying unprecedented prosperity.

For his first nine months in office, 2001, George W. Bush dealt with same old, same old: trade embargoes, illegal immigration, corporate upsizing, education, Social Security reform. Prophetically, in his first State of the Union address, President Bush urged Americans to seek community service, as if it could cure the national malaise of growing apathy about anything beyond one's front door: "I ask you to seek a common good beyond your comfort . . . to serve your nation, beginning with your neighbor. I ask you to be citizens. Citizens, not spectators. Citizens, not subjects. Responsible citizens, building communities of service and a nation of character."

And then 9/11. During the next four years the world also experienced catastrophic natural disasters. The Southeast Asian tsunami killed 275,000 people; Hurricane Katrina killed 1,281 and wiped out most of New Orleans; and the October 2005 Pakistani earthquake killed 79,000. If anything positive came out of the tragic loss of life and property from the destruction of the World Trade Center's Twin Towers and the utter devastation wrought by the natural disasters, it was the motivation to bring Americans out of their private self-absorption. Every American felt these losses as if a part of them had also died. These tragedies kindled a compassion for other Americans and for our fellow world citizens. Firefighters, police officers, emergency medical personnel, the military, and volunteers became our new heroes. After global emotional paralysis and mourning, volunteerism was up 80 percent after a 30-year decline. The U.S. Bureau of Labor Statistics counted 59 million volunteers in schools, faith-based organizations, nonprofits, and hospitals.

The country's dramatic recovery from 9/11 and its continuing recovery from Hurricane Katrina can be attributed to American optimism, resiliency, and creativity, the same qualities that characterize the volunteer. That's the fundamental reason volunteerism has always been part of the American character. Indeed, the Revolutionary War most probably would not have been won without minutemen. Colonial settlements relied exclusively on volunteer fire departments, as do many rural communities today. Inherent in the American spirit is the willingness to pitch in and help others. The 9/11 attacks and Hurricane Katrina put many volunteer contributions in the spotlight. The forty people who sacrificed their lives to save the White House or Capitol on United Airlines' Flight 93 will always epitomize volunteerism in its highest and most noble form. John Grisham donated $5 million to his home state, Mississippi, after Hurricane Katrina. Yet the need exists in myriad quiet ways—a need so prevalent and pervasive that it will never make the newspaper's front page. If each retiring boomer were to undertake one volunteer responsibility, we could improve the world. Marc Freedman has written an entire book on just that, called *Prime Time: How Baby Boomers Will Revolutionize Retirement and Transform America.*

The Senior Corps is one avenue to involvement. Through the Senior Corps, half a million Americans fifty-five and older now share their time and talents to help their communities. The three programs of Senior Corps are (1) the Foster Grandparents Program, whose participants serve one-on-one with young people who have special needs, (2) the Senior Companions Program, which trains seniors to help other seniors live independently in their homes, and (3) the Retired Senior Volunteer Program (RSVP), through which volunteers work with more than five hundred local groups to meet a wide range of community needs.

RSVP matches your personal interests and skills (coming from one or more of your multiple intelligences) with opportunities to help solve community problems. RSVP volunteers choose how and where they want to serve—from a few to over forty hours a week. RSVP volunteers provide hundreds of services, including the following noted on the Senior Corps Web site (www.seniorcorp.org): "They tutor children in reading and math, help to build houses, help get children immunized, model parenting skills to teen parents, participate in neighborhood watch programs, plan community gardens, deliver meals, offer disaster relief to victims of natural disasters, and help community organizations operate more efficiently." All volunteers receive preservice orientation and on-the-job training from the agency or organization of involvement. The Senior Corps Web site is extremely informative. It also provides links to programs in every state and includes phone, fax, and e-mail contact information for local representatives.

Senior Corps was not conceived as a result of 9/11. As a matter of fact, its three programs have been around for decades. The Foster Grandparents Program began in 1965; RSVP in 1969; and the Senior Companion Program in 1973. In 1993 the three were grouped under the title Senior Corps and became part of the portfolio of the Corporation for National and Community Service.

Senior Corps is just one of hundreds of established volunteer organizations. Others can be accessed via the Internet by searching on the key term "volunteer organizations" along with the subject of your concern ("literacy," for example). Or you can consult your local telephone yellow pages under "social service organizations" or "human service organizations." Opportunities abound—indeed, cry out for our help: mentoring children of imprisoned mothers; assisting the blind, the homeless, new immigrants, abused women, neglected children, abandoned animals; or offering your expertise in teaching, accounting, law, construction, nutrition, or counseling, to name a few.

If you choose not to work with a volunteer organization per se, you can be publicly creative by volunteering to fulfill a need you perceive in your neighborhood. If you have strong interpersonal skills, you could organize a meet-your-neighbors barbecue for your community. If you are endowed with spatial intelligence, you could volunteer to design and construct stage settings for the local elementary school's spring play. Those of you blessed with musical gifts could contribute invaluably to your church, synagogue, or mosque. Any way you do it, the commitment of millions of retired boomers will make an unprecedented, positive impact on society through volunteerism. For this reason, author Gene Cohen says older persons should be viewed as a "natural resource."

In addition to volunteerism, there are myriad opportunities to be personally creative that contribute to society. If you are verbally skilled, you could write poems for your baby grandson. If your husband has mathematical skills, he could create a computer-based tutorial for his granddaughter to learn multiplication and division. As of 2005, over six million boomers had already become grandparents, and that number is expected to quadruple during the next ten years. Being a grandparent affords an abundance of opportunities to contribute to the future. Watch how babies and children play. Help them identify and develop their gifts. Helping a friend or neighbor is also a way to express personal creativity. Perhaps your spatial intelligence could guide you in rearranging living space for an octogenarian.

Your emotional and social understanding (interpersonal and intrapersonal intelligences), which grows with time and experience (and, therefore, age), can be your creative gift that guides and empowers others—any others, at-the-moment-of-encounter others. Benjamin Franklin, for example, was almost seventy when the Revolutionary War broke out. Though he was already a celebrated statesman, he had yet to fully use his gifts of negotiating and diplomacy that would define our country and redefine the world.

To comprehend how this special human gift of the personal intelligences grows with age, compare early works with later works of authors who devoted their lives to writing. Walt Whitman, Mark Twain, and John Milton are just three examples. From 1855 to 1892, Walt Whitman published nine editions of *Leaves of Grass*. The first edition of twelve poems, published when Whitman was thirty-six, is dominated by "Song of Myself" and characterized by the bragging bravado of youth and celebration of physical love. Whitman's fifth edition, published when he was fifty-three, reflects the poet's emotional development with age. Whitman grew emotionally because he had experienced twenty more years of life—in particular, the Civil War period. From his experience as a wound dresser in a military hospital, Whitman wrote his *Drum-Taps* poems, expressing profound sympathy for human suffering. In his beautiful elegy to Lincoln, Whitman proffers the idea that a belief in the eternal and infinite is the consolation for earthly loss. It is apparent that Whitman's personal intelligences, his sensitivity to the human condition, and his capacity for compassion grew with age.

Mark Twain's writing career spanned nearly fifty years. To appreciate the development of Twain's social and emotional insight during his career, compare his early works, "The Celebrated Jumping Frog of Calaveras County," for example, with his later works, such as *The Adventures of Huckleberry Finn, The Tragedy of Pudd'nhead Wilson*, and *Letters from the Earth*. Written when Twain was twenty-eight, "Jumping Frog" is the hilarious story of how easily man can be duped. Later writings expose the greed, cruelty, and prejudice of the human race (*Huckleberry Finn*, written when Twain was fifty; *Pudd'nhead*, when he was fifty-nine; and *Letters from the Earth*, published posthumously). With his later works Twain became the conscience of America. Granted, he experienced more than his measure of disappointments and personal tragedies, which, no doubt, colored his view of humanity, but he didn't crumble under them. Instead, he used his experiences to counsel through his art. The point is: the longer you live, the more disappointments (and joys) you will experience; this is life. And the longer you live, therefore, the more your interpersonal and intrapersonal intelligences grow. If wisely used, your highly developed personal intelligences can be gifts to others.

John Milton was a recognized writer while he was still a student at Cambridge. His early poems "L'Allegro" and "Il Penseroso" celebrated the birth of Jesus and the vagaries of the human mood. Not until his final years, however, did Milton write his masterpieces, *Paradise Lost, Paradise Regained,* and *Samson Agonistes.* In the forty-five intervening years, Milton experienced three marriages, disappointment in the outcome of the British Reformation, and blindness. Sixty years of life had augmented his innate verbal talent with the gift of human experience so that he could write an epic poem "to justify the ways of God to man." His description of Satan's reason for rebellion, "pale ire, envy, and despair," is used two hundred years later by seventy-year-old Herman Melville in *Billy Budd,* his masterpiece about the clash between good and evil.

# PART FIVE

# Setting the Pace for Twenty-First-Century Second Adulthoods

## GOAL
### BE THE STARLIGHT

## OBJECTIVE 9

# Redefine Work—and Retirement

**Re•tire** **1** : to withdraw from action :RETREAT **2** : to fall back :RECEDE **3** **a** : to withdraw from use or service **b** : to put out **c** : to end

Besides "to conclude one's working or professional career," the above are other general definitions of *to retire*. No wonder boomers don't want to do it! And when we do retire, we'll redefine the applicable piece, substituting *re-begin* or r*e-create* for *conclude* so that the new definition will read, "**re•tire** : to re-begin or re-create one's working or professional career."

Or better yet, we'll retire the word *retire* altogether—along with its negative connotations—and adopt a new term. How about "**cae•su•ra** : a pause marking a rhythmic point of division, usually in the middle, in a melody or a poem"? That'll do, especially with the allusion to life as a song or poem still creating itself after the caesura. Or maybe, given that our generation is so techno, we'll co-opt the terms *reboot* or *rewire*. But the problem with these *re-* words is that they all mean repetition or something with backward reference. And that's not what boomers are going to do with retirement.

We'll do something new. We'll change the concept of retirement so it will have a whole new meaning. Beginning with this decade, labor economics and business textbooks will rewrite their sections on retirement. The new typical passage will go something

191

like this: "When the first wave of the baby-boom generation reached its sixth decade, retirement lost its rigid definition as 'the cessation of work.' The concept no longer implies a complete break with a job, business, or career. It is now understood to be any of a variety of work-schedule options." By the time our generation redefines *retirement*, it won't mean the end of anything, nor will it imply receding, retreating, or withdrawing from anything. Instead it will imply the looking ahead to a vast array of choices in a new mix of work and nonwork activities. In the process, we'll also redefine *work*.

Ah, yes, we boomers—the innovative, change-making generation that we are—would love to think that our redefinition of retirement signals a return to 1960s activism; that this change is a result of our protest against the way our parents retired; and that this is a full-circle stand against the system by our generation, which thirty-five years earlier proclaimed, through Bob Dylan, "I ain't gonna work on Maggie's farm no more."

But how can we rebel against the system when we *are* the system? Maybe we finally understand what we professed to understand so many decades ago: if you're not part of the solution, you're part of the problem. According to labor economists, *we* are the problem. Mind you, we didn't create the problem. Our parents did. They had seventy-seven million of us. But then we contributed to the problem by not contributing to the labor force as many kids as they did. The trend-predictor Cassandras are terrified that we'll all retire at the going age of 61.7 years and create a gap, a ravine, a cavern, a chasm, a black hole in the labor force that will hurl our country into economic chaos.

The *real* problem lies with the trend predictors (Gen-Xers, no doubt), who underestimate their parents. Remember their disdainful, "Why don't you guys ever act your age?" Do they think we're suddenly going to start acting our age? And which age, anyway? As noted earlier, are we talking about our feel, look, do, or interest age? No, indeed, we're not about to start acting our chronological age. These trend predictors are also basing their doomsday scenarios on historical parallels. Don't they know that no generation compares to ours? We are a nonpareil in human history. We are the healthiest, wealthiest, and wisest group ever to enter life's sixth decade. Moreover, our generation has superwomen, those women who proved they could do everything their mothers *and* fathers did (minus 1.7 kids). Where are the superwomen in all these predictions? A major reason these predictions are so gloomy is that our superwomen are not accounted for. Our generation will be part of the solution, and superwomen will lead the way. A new definition of retirement is part of the reengineering plan for the boom generation's grand second adulthood.

According to U.S. census figures and Bureau of Labor statistics, here's the situation as it appeared at the end of 2005:

- The baby-boom generation, born between 1946 and 1964, comprises 27.5 percent of the U.S. population.
- Beginning in 2006, one boomer will turn sixty every eleven seconds. By the end of that year, three and a half million boomers will be sixty.
- By 2010 one-third of the U.S. population will be fifty or older.
- If boomers follow current trends and retire (currently defined as dropping out of the workforce) at age 61.7, there will be a shortage of four to six million workers by 2010 because there aren't enough Gen-Xers to replace them.
- By 2015 workers fifty-five years old and older will constitute 20 percent of the workforce.
- By 2030 there will be three working-age adults for every person over sixty-five.

This situation, called a problem by the Cassandras, will lead to economic and political upheaval. Employers will face an employee shortage and a drain of vital skills. Our country will suffer a substantial slowdown in economic growth. The boomers' mass retirement over the next three decades will hammer the nation's already strained pension funds and deplete Social Security and Medicare.

OK, OK, so the new reality of an older population is quantifiable. But the boom generation has redefined age, and it doesn't include the adjective *old*. This is as much a part of the new reality as are all the numbers. Look back at those figures. The 2010 prediction of a labor force shortage of four to six million is based on boomers dropping out by age sixty-two. The 2030 prediction of three working-age adults for every person over sixty-five is assuming that boomers over sixty-five won't be working.

## CHALLENGE
### Retirement Is a Bore but Work Is a Treadmill

In the meantime, back on the home front, Superwoman is faced with another situation: her husband still can't find a retirement identity. He says retirement is like a job—you don't know if it suits you until you've tried it. He's tried and he's tried and he's tried, but he still "can't get no satisfaction" from full-time retirement.

He thought he'd love all that unstructured leisure time, but "time isn't leisure," he says, "if that's all you've got. I feel obsolete in my prime. I feel flushed out of the system. I'm a has-been, consigned to the rag bin of demography. I feel like I've been through the desert on a horse with no name. I can't *stand* an entire second adulthood of reading about other men's exciting lives in their challenging jobs. I *do* want to set my alarm clock for something besides tee times. I want to use my PDA for appointments again.

I want something on my weekly calendar besides Mondays at the shelter, Wednesdays with yoga [and wife], Thursdays with pre-Raphaelite painters [and wife and her girlfriends], and every day doing whatever your mother imagines a retired son-in-law should do for her. How can I say that my life was a job well done if I don't have a job? I don't even enjoy golf anymore because I don't have my job to talk about with my golf buddy. I'm too young to retire! I have an entire second adulthood ahead of me. Oh, how I wish *tempus* would *fugit* again! I want my job back!"

Gosh, at least he's expressing his feelings. But what he won't admit is that living in the same house 24/7 with a retired Superwoman teaching him homemaking skills is another reason he doesn't like retirement. Besides, she doesn't give him a paycheck at the end of the month. (Wouldn't your mother love to say, "What goes around comes around"?) He feels that what he contributed to society through his work and what he gained through its intrinsic reward outweigh the advantages of retirement.

Or maybe he realizes his nest egg needs more nesting. There will always be retirees who have to continue or go back to work, be it because of poor savings habits, large unexpected expenses, or disastrous market losses. Because of our long life expectancy and our stubborn independence, boomers need to assure themselves that they can have a comfortable lifestyle for at least four decades after turning sixty. Even if we don't have to work for the income, we still think of those exotic trips and cruises as vacations, something boomer men looked forward to as a respite from work, not from a routine of nothing but boring retirement downtime.

Regardless of whether Superwoman's husband is unwilling or financially unable to retire, he is still his work. He can't retire from himself. The fact is, Americans love their work. We always have. We search for the meaning in our lives and we find "I work *ergo sum*." It's not all about the money even though we value what our paychecks—or credit cards—buy. That Puritan work ethic is still around, even though the Puritan part isn't. We still believe that hard work is good for the soul. To be called a workaholic is a compliment in our culture. We are the developed world's leader in nonstop working. And we're proud of it.

Four decades ago the Germans boasted, "*Wir leben zu arbeiten*" (we live to work) while they condescendingly said of the French, "*Sie arbeiten zu leben*" (they work to live). Now the entire European Union works to live. The average American works nearly two thousand hours for fifty weeks a year in contrast to the German's fifteen hundred hours a year, a difference of almost three months of forty-hour workweeks. The European Union, moreover, mandates a minimum of four weeks' annual vacation for all member countries, which averages six to seven weeks yearly with their copious holidays. A thirty-five-hour workweek is standard in France. The average American takes only 10.2 days' vacation yearly. We even work about three weeks more a year than the Japanese. Forty percent of Americans work fifty-hour workweeks. We're proud of being busy, being productive, being our work.

Boomers, in particular, are work-happy. In 1952 and again in 1958 we saw the first two re-releases of Disney's first animated film, *Snow White and the Seven Dwarfs*. We absorbed the seven dwarfs' enthusiasm for work as we remember their singing, "Heigh-ho, heigh-ho, it's off to work we go." Is it any wonder that we can't let go of our work and so we take it with us on an electronic leash (e-mail, laptop, cell phone) when we go on our "working vacations"? Americans work long hours not just to make money. Because working is valued in our culture, we derive recognition, self-esteem, and a sense of belonging (being part of a team) from our work and workplace.

But then hubby remembers why he retired in the first place—the treadmill, being scheduled from 8 a.m. to 6 p.m. five days a week. So, what is a mover-and-shaker boomer to do after buying into the idea that success is a marathon, not a sprint? Superwoman to the rescue! She realizes that somewhere between the life of the Samurai and the Ronin there's got to be a compromise in the workplace for her husband. Maybe second-adulthood success is one more sprint to the finish line, or a walking marathon, or maybe it's a power-walking 10 K. The choice will be ours.

## STRATEGY

### Combine Retirement and Work

As leader-manager in the reengineering of their lifestyles, Superwoman searches for creative solutions. She is faced with an unhappy husband (literally, all day long) because retirement doesn't do it for him. He keeps thinking back on the meaning and purpose—and heavy stress—of the job he left. He maintains that his giftedness was expressed in his job. What's wrong with that? Nothing. As a matter of fact, the boomers' unwillingness to retire (as in drop out of the workforce) will help solve the impending disaster forecast by the labor economists.

Superwoman's strategy here is to dissolve the boundary between work and retirement. Why shouldn't the generation that invented the working vacation be the generation to invent the working retirement? She is aware that some boomers—especially leading-edge male boomers—can't find fulfillment in hearth and home, all-day play, and volunteerism. Because she has used Gardner's definition of giftedness, she realizes that her husband's love of his work is an expression of his passion, a chance to use his skills and talents in one or in a combination of the eight forms of giftedness.

Together Superwoman and her husband review the last part of their vision for second adulthood: "We accept the obligations of discovering our unique gifts and of contributing positively to society. We will set the pace in redefining the human experience." Surely, our unique gifts can be manifested in new or enhanced careers. "Contributing positively to society"? Given all the doomsday stats, we certainly can contribute to society by working longer and by inventing a working retirement. "Setting the pace in redefining the human experience"? As a generational cohort, we have already redefined our culture as we moved through each passage in our lives. We are still redefining social conscience, lifestyle, and vitality. Now we shall redefine retirement.

We first-wave boomers are in a position to be the starlight for the rest of our generation and for the generations to follow. We have the opportunity to redefine what it means to retire. Actually, we've already expressed our desires. According to a recent AARP survey, 80 percent of boomers expect to work at least part-time during retirement, 17 percent say they intend to start a business, and 5 percent say they'll look for full-time work in a new career. Moreover, typical boomers say they expect to retire from their current full-time job at age sixty-seven. This desire to delay the age of retirement is driven by a number of factors, uppermost being the boomers' love of work. Additionally, studies have shown that working longer at something you love is linked to physical and mental health in later years.

As leader-manager in the couple's reengineering for a fulfilling second adulthood, Superwoman guides the search for current and emerging options for working retirements. Companies that think ahead are already making changes that will enable them to retain older workers instead of getting rid of them. The demographic facts that eighteen million boomers will have turned sixty and one-third of the U.S. population will be fifty or older in 2010 is the elephant in the boardroom. Progressive companies are offering incentives to delay the departure of seasoned employees. This is a dramatic and rapid change from the corporate downsizing climate of just a decade ago, when anyone past fifty became a target for showing to the door, and the door prize was the early retirement package.

Now the corporate mind-set is focusing on how to retain older workers because we are an asset. The thinking is that we are healthy, educated, reliable, and experienced, and so we are well suited for jobs that require seasoned judgment and reason—jobs such as mentoring and training new employees, counseling, long-range planning, and arbitration. In addition, we have a good work ethic, and we can be used as a marketing tool for a boomer customer base that relates to its contemporaries.

For the 80 percent of boomers who say they expect to continue working at least part-time, there are these emerging options:

- **Work/life arrangements,** in which employers keep and cultivate loyal employees by having on-site personal benefits such as gyms, cafés, secure and dedicated parking lots, workshops and counseling in the areas of health and finance, and so on.
- **Corporate alumni networks,** also called on-call retirees, wherein retired employees are asked to stay connected to their former employer and be available for reemployment if needed. Specialists who have retired may be called in to work on short-term projects and be paid based on their former salary although ineligible for benefits.
- **Phased retirement,** an arrangement whereby employees might postpone total retirement by cutting back gradually. This arrangement, however, creates major problems under current pension, labor, and tax laws. These problems will be dealt with in the near future as boomers demand changes. Uncle Sam is not about to let himself be done in. Age dis-

crimination, for example, is already outlawed. The age of
Social Security eligibility has been incrementally raised.

- **Part-time or seasonal work,** which is the ideal mode of
working retirement that most boomers envision, according
to a recent New Retirement Survey by Merrill Lynch and
Harris Interactive. This arrangement involves repeated
cycles of periods of work alternating with periods of
leisure.
- **Job sharing,** wherein two employees share everything
about a job—its workload, its salary, and most of its benefits. One or the other employee must be willing to do
without the healthcare benefit.
- **Temporary staffing,** in which a worker retires one day and
comes back the next, but now on the payroll of a tempo-
rary-help agency.
- **Consulting,** when retirees are rehired as independent-con-
tractor consultants by the business they retired from
(which frees the consultant to take other consulting jobs
as well).
- **Working at home,** an arrangement often preferred as more
productive than office-based work by businesses that rely
on telecommuting or Web-based connections with their
clientele.

Since the year 2000, AARP has published its annual list "Best
Employers for Workers over 50." In addition, AARP's Featured
Employers program highlights companies that have different jobs
available that require different skills and offer different benefits.
Some want full-time workers; others, seasonal or part-time all-year
employees. Go to www.AARP.org/featuredemployers and click on
the name of each employer for basic information about the
company.

Recognizing the need for seasoned scientists, Proctor & Gamble and Eli Lilly founded YourEncore in 2003 "to connect the R&D and product development needs of member companies with retirees who have a wealth of scientific and technical background."

Senior JobBank is a "nonprofit referral service dedicated to keeping older people in the workplace longer. Senior JobBank offers free employment referrals for job seekers over 50. Listings include occasional, part-time, temporary, and full-time employment opportunities."

The experts warn of impending staffing shortages in critical fields, particularly education, health care, and social services. If the shortages could be offset by the growing supply of boomers who say they want second-adulthood jobs that help people, we would have a labor economist's dream. We would certainly replace the label *me-generation* with *re-generation*. We also need to be vigilant in encouraging the U.S. Labor Department to amend employment laws to make it easier for employers to implement incentives to entice and hold onto older—strike that, *seasoned*—workers.

---

## OBJECTIVE 10

## *Seize Your Re-Generation*

They seem like a mere nanosecond, those six decades of our lives so far. But in that micron on civilization's time line, we've made more change than any generation in history. The boom generation created more information in the past thirty years than humankind created in the previous five thousand. Ten billion pages of online text are now searchable via Internet search engines. In the next half decade, today's information quantity will double, and it will include videos and photographic images in searchable digital format. It's as if the starship *Enterprise* had transported us—at warp speed—out of the industrial era into the information age.

What technology holds in store for us is predictable because technology deals with things—or at least ideas that apply to things—that are quantifiable. Futurists make predictions based on current trends. But these predictions don't always follow the formula or the graph. Why not? Because of the unpredictable human factor. Remember the prediction in the late 1970s that computers would make us a paperless society by the turn of the century? Well, by the turn of the century we were consuming 115 billion sheets of paper annually for personal computers, with a 50 percent increase in worldwide paper consumption expected by 2010. In the meantime, our paper consumption is to blame for global deforestation and bulging landfills. Futurists couldn't predict the human need for the printed word—the ultimate backup and the adult substitute for our babyhood security blanket, the hard copy.

Yes, the human factor makes the final outcomes of social trends very hard to predict with accuracy. Futurists attempt to predict what human beings will do tomorrow based on their behavior in analogous circumstances in the past. And this is precisely why *no one* can predict what the baby-boom generation will do with its future. No generation has entered its seventh decade in such vast numbers with so much education and promise of healthy longevity. We have always eluded the predictions because we were making unprecedented change as we passed through every stage of our lives. But there's one thing about the boom generation that you sure enough can count on: we will continue to make change. Big change. Positive change.

We've always been the new guy on the block. In 1946 we swelled maternity wards right into the hospital corridors when our births jumped five and a half million over the number of births the year before. A decade later we were forcing unprepared schools into double sessions. We tripled college enrollments between 1965 and 1975. And along the way we were heralding sweeping changes that brought equal educational and social opportunities for all American citizens, regardless of their race or sex.

Out of this opportunity, of course, emerged superwomen, the women of all colors, ethnicities, and religions who became a new change-making force for the United States. For the first time in human history they redefined marriage by removing *obey* from the vow of *love, honor, and obey*. In its place they have shared with their spouses a pledge of mutual respect.

With her spouse, Superwoman has now entered a new stage of life and is rising to the new challenge. She is again breaking ground in uncharted territory, for herself, for her generation, and for all the generations to follow. As motivator, team leader, change agent, and coach (remember, never boss), she has written a blueprint to accomplish the reengineering of an entire generation as it enters a second adulthood.

Superwoman breathes a sigh of happiness and relief as she reflects on the road that has brought her now, with husband, to the achievement of the final objective (seizing your re-generation). She remembers how retirement from first-adulthood jobs marked the transition into second-adulthood life. After getting hubby's buy-in with the vision statement for retirement, Superwoman structured goals and objectives that would fulfill the vision. Her strategy for change was built around her baby-boom generation's first-adulthood values and the related challenges she and her husband would confront, and would change into opportunities, as they grew and developed into their second adulthoods.

Superwoman realized that the transition offered more challenges to her husband than to herself because of his job-based identity, because of post–World War II redefinitions of his role in marriage, and because of some hardwired maleness. Indeed, the road from top executive to happily retired spouse wouldn't be a straight path. There were sure to be curves ahead, falling rocks, and Sirens luring him into daily tee times. Fortunately, this boom-generation Odysseus had and still has Superwoman as Athena guiding his journey and ensuring his success. (Gosh, that means Superwoman is also Odysseus' faithful, loving wife, Penelope. But that's all right; Superwoman is used to multitasking. That's why *she* wrote this guide in the first place.)

In the end, this particular boomer couple will achieve all ten objectives. In analyzing Objective 9, Redefine Work—and Retirement, however, Superwoman realized that she failed to create a completely new hearth-and-home identity for her husband. But that's acceptable because he took on a new job-based identity that drew on his giftedness in new ways, and his new work arrangement structured his time and gave his life renewed purpose. Superwoman says she may revisit the reengineering for hearth-and-home identity for her husband's third adulthood, which is nowhere in the foreseeable future.

In the meantime, this leading-edge boomer couple are relishing their second adulthood. They're giving and getting love in their relationships with each other, their parents, their children, and their friends. They're physically fit and look like their feel, do, and interest ages. As ambassadors for world understanding, they're working with their global neighbors. They're adding zest to their lives by learning new things, and they're experiencing the joy that comes from expressing their creativity. Finally, they are experiencing spiritual fulfillment in knowing they are contributing positively to society through their citizen stewardship and volunteerism.

## CHALLENGE
### Routine Is Comfortable

Change, once accomplished and implemented, is no longer change. It becomes the status quo. Even a successful transition into second adulthood can melt down to routine. Routine is comfortable, the easier road in our life's journey. But the boom generation always chose the road less traveled. We've taken risks. We've *made* change, not succumbed to it as a force outside our control. It's tempting now to look back and say, "Look what I've accomplished. I had a successful first adulthood. I've just reengineered myself for my second adulthood. Now I can settle into my new lifestyle for the next several decades. No more bumps in my road." What's wrong with this thinking? Routine is deceptive. It's comfortable at first; then it becomes deadly boring. Actually, it can also become deadly.

Second adulthood offers a new choice of roads, and one is the road never before traveled by a generation. It has milestones never seen before. Its signs may read "construction zone," "detour," or "yield to merging generations," but we will interpret these signs as challenges and part of the adventure, not as roadblocks on our new journey. Poets and prophets speak anew to our generation with their cautionary tales and verses about life squandered. The gift of second adulthood is like receiving the talents in the biblical parable. We can use this gift or ignore it. If we ignore it, we condemn ourselves to what Thoreau described as a life of "quiet desperation [which is] confirmed resignation"; what Edgar Lee Masters described as "a boat longing for the sea and yet afraid . . . leading a life without meaning [in] the torture of restlessness and vague desire"; and what T. S. Eliot described as the "shadow" that falls between the "motion and the act"—we condemn ourselves to lives that end in "a whimper." No; just as we boast about our first adulthood's road, we want to be able to quote Robert Frost and say of our second adulthood's road, "I took the one never before traveled, and that has made all the difference."

## STRATEGY
### Seek Continuous Improvement

Superwoman and her husband embrace the core value that says significant people grow and change throughout their lives. They accomplish this growth through self-examination, communication, turning problems into opportunities, and setting goals. Put succinctly, they eschew bystanderism. They believe that their choices determine who they are. They also believe that every human being is here on this planet for some unique purpose, some noble objective. If we haven't found our purpose yet, now is the opportunity.

Second adulthood is a blessing bestowed on our generation. It is a blessing because it is a second chance to live these core values, an opportunity to change forever what it means to live, retire, and age in modern America. Collectively, we can undo our spoiled, self-absorbed, and self-indulgent me-generation reputation of entitlement and put personal accountability back in style.

As Gregg Easterbrook says in *Progress Paradox: How Life Gets Better While People Feel Worse*, we have a duty, an obligation to those who came before us, to live our lives with gratitude and optimism:

> Hundreds of generations who came before us lived dire, short lives, in deprivation or hunger, in ignorance or under oppression or during war, and did so partly motivated by the dream that someday there would be men and women who lived long lives in liberty with plenty to eat and without fear of an approaching storm.

> Suffering through privation, those who came before us accumulated the knowledge that makes our lives favored; fought the battles that made our lives free; physically built much of what we rely on for our prosperity; and, most important, shaped the ideals of liberty. For all the myriad problems of modern society, we now live in the world our forefathers would have wished for us—in many ways, a better place than they dared imagine. For us not to feel grateful is treacherous selfishness.

As the meat in the intergenerational sandwich, don't we also have a duty to pass this attitude on to our children and our children's children?

Because we're the first generation to enjoy second adulthoods in a country experiencing an unprecedented standard of living, we have choices that humankind has never before been offered. Would it be better to start our own business, become a consultant, or return to work on our terms? Should we write a book or teach part-time? Should we become foster grandparents or offer to mentor at the homeless shelter? Should we plan adventure, ecology, or philanthropy travel? Should we start a recycling program in our community, buy a hybrid car, change a former dump site into a beautifully landscaped park? Should we volunteer to teach immigrant children reading, or join the Senior Corps and teach children in a developing country? Should we take golf lessons so we can play with our husbands?

Whatever choices boomers make for their second adulthoods, we should aim for the final stage of reengineering: continuous improvement. We can always get better. Choices also imply distinctions between ethical and unethical, moral and immoral, short-term sacrifice for long-term reward. It is incumbent upon us as twenty-first-century leaders to set the pace in making the right choices. We have the gifts of time, security, and accumulated wisdom to become the starlight guiding future generations.

All this time your echo-boomer children have been curiously observing you get reengineered. Now when they hear your plans, they venture, "Wow! You have all this planned for your second adulthood? What are you going to do in your dotage?"

To which Superwoman answers, "Dotage? Oh, you mean *dot age*, as in *dot com, dot org,* and *dot net*. I've planned a blog for male boomers, and . . . *Oh, please,* would someone create a retirement simulation videogame for boom-generation men? It could be titled "Baby, You Ain't Seen Nothin' Yet!"

Look! Up in the sky! It's . . . oh, it couldn't be. It must be a shooting star.

# Acknowledgments

I am grateful for the opportunity to write this book. But how does one thank opportunity? I do this by thanking the people behind the opportunity.

Foremost is Meredith Rutter, publisher for VanderWyk & Burnham. Meredith said "yes" to my unagented, unsolicited proposal from an unknown author. Since then, she has been encouraging, constructively critical, and patient. She is blessed with the gift—or skill—of always sounding affirmative when I know I deserved otherwise. In short, Meredith Rutter personifies what her publishing house is all about: making a difference in people's lives. She certainly has in mine.

Secondly, I thank Ethel Danhof, former colleague and friend on the highest level of Aristotle's definition of friendship. Ethel was the angel-on-my-shoulder throughout this project. Not only did she see me through the clouds of self-doubt, she also epitomizes what second adulthood is all about.

For tolerance of how his project left my other responsibilities undone, I thank my husband, Ed, who now considers himself the specimen. If it were not for his anchoring much of what Superwoman formerly anchored, I could not have written this book. For my perspective on the echo-boomer generation, I thank my son, Spencer, and his friends. May the force be with you.

I thank my parents for availing me the opportunity to be all that my place in human history said I could be. My mother and father will always be part of who I am. I thank my mother-in-law, Anna Floyd, a strong and affirmative survivor of the "greatest generation," who never said I should be less.

I am grateful to every source in my bibliography because these people, institutions, and government agencies are paving the way for the baby-boom generation's second adulthood.

Finally, I acknowledge all 17.4 million superwomen of my generation, particularly those with whom I have had the privilege of working. I admire and respect you.

# Notes

## Introduction

**Page xiii**: **The boom generation's retirement is the subject of studies...** Health Services Research..., Knickman and Snell, "The 2030 Problem: Caring for Aging Baby Boomers." / **Congressional Budget Office...**, Congressional Budget Office, "Projections of the Labor Force, September 2004." / **Economic Policy Institute...**, Baker, "Defusing the Baby Boomer Time Bomb: Projections of Income in the 21st Century." / **National Institute on Aging...**, National Institute on Aging, "Alzheimer's Disease Neuroimaging Study Launched Nationwide." / **AARP...**, Roper Starch Worldwide, Inc., *Baby Boomers Envision Their Retirement: An AARP Segmentation Analysis, 1999.* [Roper Starch conducted this study for AARP.] / **Stanford...**, Stanford University, "Baby Boomers Face Uncertainty Regarding Retirement Income." [Stanford University economist John Shoven forecasts the future of America's private pension system as the boom generation retires and withdraws pensions.] / **Cornell...**, Lang, "New Book Explores Problems of Health Coverage and Income Security as Aging Baby Boomers Approach Retirement." [This Cornell News release reviews the book *Ensuring Health and Security for an Aging Workforce* published by the W. E. Upjohn Institute for Employment Research (2001) and co-edited by Richard Burkhauser, professor of policy analysis and management at Cornell University.]

## Part One: Superwoman Leads the Way!

**Page 4**: **Tom Brokaw's "greatest generation"...**, Brokaw, *The Greatest Generation.*

## Part Two: Getting a New Identity in Real Time

**Page 15**: **We became adults believing that faster...**, discussion of time in this and the next paragraph drawn from Gleich, *Faster: The Acceleration of Just About Everything.* / **Page 33**: **"carrying heavy buckets of water...,"** Cowan, *More Work for Mother*, 166.

## Part Three: Giving and Getting Love

**Page 50**: **"Tell me what'd I say"...**, Charles, "What'd I Say," 1959. / **Page 58**: **"You make me wanna (shout!)"...**, Isley Brothers, "Shout!," 1959. / **Simon and Garfunkel sang the warnings...**, Simon, "Sound of Silence," 1964. / **Page 59**: **Women share their feelings...**, Tannen, *You Just Don't Understand.*

[Deborah Tannen, a professor of linguistics at Georgetown University, was one of the first to write a guidebook explaining the difference between men and women's expectations of conversation. This and the following paragraphs give a brief overview of what relationship experts say about the disparity in communication between the sexes.] / **Page 60**: **John Gray says it's the way people are wired...**, Gray, *Men Are from Mars, Women Are from Venus,* and *Mars and Venus Together Forever.* / **Leslie Brody and Judith Hall say the pattern is set early...**, Brody and Hall, "Gender and Emotion," 454–456. / **Robert and Beverly Cairns trace men's and women's differing expectations...**, Cairns, *Lifelines and Risks.* / **Page 61**: **Daniel Goleman attributes to nature *and* nurture...**, Goleman, *Emotional Intelligence,* 133. / **Page 70**: **In your search for solutions, you consult Michael Gurian's...**, Gurian, "What's in His Head: A Friendly Look at the Male Brain," 3–32. / **Page 73**: **Start with Stephen Covey's fifth habit...to manipulate"...**, Covey, *The Seven Habits of Highly Effective People,* 240. [Covey's analysis of the autobiographical response is used here because he offers a strategy for conquering it.] / **Covey defines four varieties of autobiographical responses...,"** Covey, 245. / **Page 74**: **As an antidote to listening autobiographically...**, Covey, 248–249. / **Page 75**: **As Barbra Streisand sings, "With one person...,"** Merrill, "People," 1963. / **Page 79**: **"You're the cream...lost without you!"...**, DeSylva et al, "You're the Cream in My Coffee," 1928. / **Page 89**: **Financial journalist Jane Bryant Quinn...**, Quinn, *Making the Most of Your Money,* 27–32. / **Page 93**: **...the needs that Medicare.gov...**, Medicare.gov, Long Term Care. "Steps to Choosing Long-Term Care." / **Page 95**: **...Green Houses founded by Dr. William H. Thomas...**, Thomas, *What Are Old People For?,* 222–235. / **According to the MetLife Mature Market Institute...**, MetLife Mature Market Institute, *The MetLife Market Survey of Assisted Living Costs,* 7. / **If they do, you can hire a home health aide...**, MetLife Mature Market Institute, maturemarketinstitute.com, "Home Health Aide." / **The National Council on Aging notes...**, National Council on Aging, "Caregiving: Caregivers and Care Recipients." / **Page 105**: **"Have You Never Been Mellow?"...**, Farrar, "Have You Never Been Mellow," 1975. / **Page 109**: **"Find out what they like...,"** Waller and Razaf, "Find Out What They Like and How They Like It," 1929. / **Page 113**: **A ten-year study at Flinders University...**, Giles et al, "Effect of Social Networks on 10 Year Survival in Very Old Australians," 574–579. / **Page 115**: **...Wordsworth's "Tintern Abbey"..."that best...of love,"** Wordsworth, "Lines Composed a Few Miles above Tintern Abbey," 108.

Part Four: Reengineering Your Lifestyle

Page 123: The product was HGH..., Federal Trade Commission, "FCT Targets Bogus Anti-Aging Claims for Pills and Sprays Promising Human Growth Hormone Benefits." / Page 128: The 2005 Food Pyramid recommends..., Department of Health and Human Services and United States Department of Agriculture, *Dietary Guidelines for Americans, 2005*. [This is an 80-page report that gives "science-based advice on food and physical activity choices for health." It is part of the 2005 MyPyramid website accessible at MyPyramid.gov "Inside the Pyramid" as well as existing as a separate document published by Health and Human Services and the Department of Agriculture.] / Page 130: Surgeon General Carmona says obesity..., Tumulty, "The Politics of Fat," 41. / Page 141: For overweight adults, My Pyramid recommends..., United States Department of Agriculture, MyPyramid.gov "Inside the Pyramid," "How much physical activity is needed?" / Page 144: "Why is physical activity important?"..., United States Department of Agriculture, MyPyramd.gov "Inside the Pyramid," "Why is physical activity important?" / Page 146: ...the rundown on exercise from *Dietary Guidelines 2005*..., chart from Chapter 4, "Physical Activity" at http://www.mypyramid.gov/pyramid/calories_used_table.html. / Page 149: In 2005 nearly 400 obesity-related bills...Huckabee...program nationwide, Tumulty, "The Politics of Fat," 41–43. / Likewise, former president Bill Clinton..., Kluger, "How Bill Put the Fizz in the Fight Against Fat," 22–25. / Page 154: To our generation, with an estimated annual spending..., MetLife Mature Market Institute, "Estimated Annual Spending Power of the Baby Boomers Is More Than $2 Trillion." / The web sites of the American Society of Plastic Surgeons..., www.plasticsurgery.org. / ...American Society for Aesthetic Plastic Surgery..., www.surgery.org. / Page 157: ...consults *Man's Search for Ultimate Meaning*..., Frankl, *Man's Search for Ultimate Meaning*, 138–142. / Page 162: The Teaching Company..., The Teaching Company's catalogs can be accessed at www.TEACH12.com or by calling 1-800-832-2412. / Page 163: As James Truslow Adams said, "There are...to live," James Truslow Adams quotes, ThinkExist.com Quotations. / Page 166: In *The Collapse of the Common Good* Philip Howard said..., Howard, *The Collapse of the Common Good*, 200. / Pages 175–177: "The first kind of smart...rather than with others," Armstrong, "Many Kinds of Minds" from *7 Kinds of Smart*, 9–11. / Page 177: Gardner's eighth intelligence is *naturalist*..., Gardner, *The Disciplined Mind*, 147–149, 154–158. / Page 178: "I left the woods...", Thoreau, *Walden*, from *The American Tradition in Literature*,

1199. / **Page 179**: Gene Cohen, an expert in tapping creative potential…, Cohen, *The Creative Age*, 28–32. / …collectively called "emotional intelligence"…, Goleman, *Emotional Intelligence*, 268. / **Page 184**: Marc Freedman has written an entire book…, Freedman, *Prime Time*. / The Senior Corps is one avenue…, Corporation for National and Community Service, www.seniorcorps.gov/about/programs/rsvp.asp. / **Page 186**: …author Gene Cohen says…"natural resource," Cohen, *The Creative Age*, 278. / As of 2005, over 6 million boomers…, United States Small Business Administration, "A Profile of Baby Boomers at Mid-Decade," www.sba.gov/gopher/Business-Development/Success-Stories/Vol10.

**Part Five: Setting the Pace for Twenty-First-Century Second Adulthoods**
**Page 192**: "I ain't gonna work on Maggie's farm no more," Dylan, "Maggie's Farm," 1965. / **Page 193**: According to U.S. census figures…, United States Census Bureau, "Age Data, Baby Boomer." / …Bureau of Labor statistics…, United States Department of Labor, "BLS Releases 2004-14 Employment Projections." / **Page 198**: According to a recent AARP survey, 80 percent of boomers…, Roper Starch Worldwide, "Baby Boomers Envision Their Retirement: An AARP Segmentation Analysis." / **Page 200**: Part-time or seasonal work…, Merrill Lynch, et al, "New Retirement Survey." / **Page 201**: Recognizing the need for seasoned scientists…"to connect…background," Proctor & Gamble and Eli Lilly, YourEncore, Inc., www.yourencore.com. / Senior JobBank is a "nonprofit referral service…opportunities," www.senior-jobbank.org. [Senior JobBank describes itself as a "meeting place for over-50 job seekers and employers seeking their services.] / **Page 202**: …consuming 115 billion sheets of paper annually…, Sevin, "Paper Chase," *Grist Magazine*. / **Page 205**: …we condemn our selves to what…Thoreau described as…, Thoreau, *Walden*, 1156. / Edgar Lee Masters described as…, Masters, "George Gray," 87. / T. S. Eliot described as…, Eliot, "The Hollow Men," 58–59. / …we want to be able to quote Robert Frost…, Frost, "The Road Not Taken," 668. / **Page 206**: As Gregg Easterbrook says…, Easterbrook, *The Progress Paradox*, 242–243.

# Bibliography and Credits

Armstrong, Thomas. "Many Kinds of Minds," from 7 KINDS OF SMART by Thomas Armstrong, copyright © 1993 by Thomas Armstrong. Used by permission of Plume, an imprint of Penguin Group (USA) Inc.

Baker, Dean. "Defusing the Baby Boomer Time Bomb: Projections of Income in the 21st Century," EPI Releases New Report, July 6, 1998, Executive Summary. http://www.commondreams.org/pressreleases/July98/070698c.htm

Brody, Leslie R., and Judith A. Hall. "Gender and Emotion," *Handbook of Emotions*. Edited by Michael Lewis and Jeannette Haviland. New York: Guilford Press, 1993.

Brokaw, Tom. *The Greatest Generation*. New York: Random House, 2004.

Cairns, Robert B., and Beverly D. Cairns. *Lifelines and Risks*. New York: Cambridge University Press, 1994.

Charles, Ray, "What'd I Say." Unichappell Music and Mijac Music, 1959.

Cohen, Gene D. *The Creative Age: Awakening Human Potential in the Second Half of Life*. New York: Avon Books, 2000. Used with permission.

Congressional Budget Office. *Projections of the Labor Force, September 2004.* http://www.cbo.gov/ftpdocs/58xx/doc5803/09-15-LaborForce.pdf

Covey, Stephen. From THE SEVEN HABITS OF HIGHLY EFFECTIVE PEOPLE by Stephen R. Covey. Copyright © 1989 by Stephen R. Covey. Reprinted by permission of Simon and Schuster Adult Publishing Group.

Cowan, Ruth Schwartz. *More Work for Mother: The Ironies of Household Technology from Open Hearth to the Microwave*. New York: Basic Books, 1983.

Department of Health and Human Services and United States Department of Agriculture. *Dietary Guidelines for Americans, 2005.* www.healthierus.gov/dietaryguidelines/index.html.

DeSylva, B.G., Lew Brown, and Ray Henderson. YOU'RE THE CREAM IN MY COFFEE. Words and Music by B.G. DESYLVA, LEW BROWN, and RAY HENDERSON. © 1928 (Renewed) DESYLVA, BROWN, and HENDERSON, INC.

Rights for the Extended Renewal Term in the United States Controlled by RAY HENDERSON MUSIC COMPANY, CHAPPELL & CO., and STEPHEN BALLENTINE MUSIC. Rights for Canada controlled by CHAPPELL & CO. All Rights Reserved. Used by Permission.

Dylan, Bob. "Maggie's Farm." 1965.

Easterbrook, Gregg. *The Progress Paradox: How Life Gets Better While People Feel Worse.* New York: Random House, 2003. Used with permission.

Eliot, T.S. "The Hollow Men," *The Complete Poems and Plays: 1909–1950.* New York: Harcourt, Brace & World, 1971.

Farrar, John. "Have You Never Been Mellow" by John Farrar. © 1975 Jumbuck Music Ltd. Used by permission. All Rights Reserved. International Copyright Secured.

Federal Trade Commission. "FTC Targets Bogus Anti-Aging Claims for Pills and Sprays Promising Human Growth Hormone Benefits: Settlement Provides Up to $20 Million in Consumer Redress." June 9, 2005. http://www.ftc.gov/opa/2005/06greatamerican.htm.

Frankl, Viktor. *Man's Search for Ultimate Meaning.* New York: Perseus Publishing, 2000. Used with permission.

Freedman, Marc. *Prime Time: How Baby Boomers Will Revolutionize Retirement and Transform America.* New York: Public Affairs, 2002.

Frost, Robert. "The Road Not Taken," *American Poetry.* Edited by Gay Wilson Allen, Walter B. Rideout, and James K. Robinson. New York: Harper & Row, 1965.

Gardner, Howard. *The Disciplined Mind: Beyond Facts and Standardized Tests, the K–12 Education That Every Child Deserves.* New York: Penguin, 2000.

Giles, Lynne C., Gary F.V. Glonek, Mary A. Luszcz, and Gary R. Andrews. "Effect of Social Networks on 10 Year Survival in Very Old Australians: The Australian Longitudinal Study of Aging" *Journal of Epidemiology and Community Health 2005;* 59:574–579. © 2005 BMJ Publishing Group Ltd. http://jech.bmjjournals.com/cgi/content/abstract/59/7/574. Study summary in "People with Many Friends Outlive Those with Few Friends by 22 Percent." http:seniorliving.about.com/od/lifetransitionsaging/a/longevity.htm.

Gleich, James. *Faster: The Acceleration of Just About Everything.* New York: Vintage Books, 2000.

Goleman, Daniel. *Emotional Intelligence.* New York: Bantam Books, 1994.

Gray, John. *Mars and Venus Together Forever: A Practical Guide to Creating Lasting Intimacy.* New York: Harper Paperbacks, 1994.

-----. *Men Are from Mars, Women Are from Venus.* New York: HarperCollins, 1992.

Gurian, Michael. "What's in His Head: A friendly Look at the Male Brain," *What Could He Be Thinking? How a Man's Mind Really Works.* New York: St. Martin's Press, 2003.

Howard, Philip K. *The Collapse of the Common Good: How America's Lawsuit Culture Undermines Our Freedom.* New York: Ballantine Books, 2000.

Isley Brothers, "Shout!" EMI Longitude Music Co., 1959.

Kluger, Jeffrey. "How Bill Put the Fizz in the Fight Against Fat," *Time Magazine* (May 15, 2006): 22–25.

Knickman, James R., & Emily K. Snell. "The 2030 Problem: Caring for Aging Baby Boomers," *Health Services Research* 37 (4), 849–884. doi: 10.1034/j.1600-0560.2002.56.x. http://www.blackwellsynergy.com/links/doi/10.1034/j.16000-0560.2002.56.x

Lang, Susan S. "New Book Explores Problems of Health Coverage and Income Security as Aging Baby Boomers Approach Retirement." News Release, October 4, 2001. http://www.news.cornell.edu/releases/Oct01/burkhauser.book.ssl.html.

Masters, Edgar Lee. "George Gray," *Spoon River Anthology.* New York: Collier Books, 1962.

Medicare.gov. Long Term Care. "Steps to Choosing Long-Term Care." http://www.medicare.gov/LongTermCare/Static/Step1.asp?dest=NAV%7CSteps%7CSteps . . .

Merrill, Bob. PEOPLE. Words by BOB MERRILL. Music by JULE STYNE. © 1963, 1964 (Renewed) BOB MERRILL and JULE STYNE. All Rights Administered by CHAPPELL & CO., INC. All Rights Reserved. Used by Permission.

Merrill Lynch, Harris Interactive, and Ken Dychtwald of Age Wave. *The New Retirement Survey*. February 22, 2005. http://askmerrill.ml.com/html/ mlrr_learn/ . . .

MetLife Mature Market Institute. *The MetLife Market Survey of Assisted Living Costs*. Westport, CT: Mature Market Institute, October 2005. Used with permission.

-----. MatureMarketInstitute.com. Demographic Profile of American Baby Boomers. "Estimated Annual Spending Power of the Baby Boomers Is More Than $2 trillion." May 24, 2005. http://www.maturemarketinsti tute.com

-----. MatureMarketInstitute.com. *The MetLife Market Survey of Assisted Living Costs*, "Home Health Aide." http://www.maturemarketinstitute.com

National Council on Aging. "Caregiving: Caregivers and Care Recipients." http://www.ncoa.org/content.cfm?sectionID=103&detail=1180

National Institute on Aging. "Alzheimer's Disease Neuroimaging Study Launched Nationwide by the National Institutes of Health." Press Release, February 9, 2006. http://www.nia.nih.gov/NewsAndEvents/PressReleases/ PR20060209ADNI.htm.

Quinn, Jane Bryant. *Making the Most of Your Money: Completely Revised and Updated for the Twenty-First Century*. New York: Simon & Schuster, 1997.

Roper Starch Worldwide. *Baby Boomers Envision Their Retirement: An AARP Segmentation Analysis, 1999*. http://www.aarp.org/research/reference/ publicopinions/aresearch-import-229.html.

Sevin, Josh. "Paper Chase," *Grist Magazine*, February 2, 2000. http://www.grist.org/news/counter/2000/02/02/paper . . .

Simon, Paul. "Sound of Silence," 1964. "Maggie's Farm," 1965.

Stanford University. "Baby Boomers Face Uncertainty Regarding Retirement Income." News Release, February 1, 1995. http://www.stanford.edu/ dept/news/pr/95/950201Arc5394.html.

Tannen, Deborah. *You Just Don't Understand: Men and Women in Conversation*. New York: Ballentine Books, 1990.

ThinkExist.com Quotations. "James Truslow Adams quotes." ThinkExist.com Quotations Online 1 Feb. 2006. 15 Mar. 2006. http://en.thinkexist.com/quotes/james_truslow_adams/ Used with permission.

Thomas, William H. *What Are Old People For? How Elders Will Save the World.* Acton, MA: VanderWyk & Burnham, 2004.

Thoreau, Henry David. *Walden.* Vol.1, *The American Tradition in Literature.* Edited by Sculley Bradley, Richmond Beatty, and E. Hudson Long. New York: W.W. Norton & Company, 1962.

Tumulty, Karen. "The Politics of Fat," *Time Magazine* (March 17, 2006): 41–43.

United States Census Bureau. Age Data. Baby Boomer. http://www.census.gov/population/www/socdemo/age.html

United States Department of Agriculture. MyPyramid.gov. Inside the Pyramid. "How much physical activity is needed?" http://www.mypyrmid.gov/pyramid/physical_activity_amount.html.

-----. MyPyramid.gov. Inside the Pyramid. "Why is physical activity important?" http://www.mypyramid.gov/pyramid/physical_activity_amount.html.

United States Department of Labor. Bureau of Labor Statistics. "BLS Releases 2004-14 Employment Projections." http://www.bls.gov/news.release/eco-pro.nr0.htm.

United States Small Business Administration. Business Development, Success Series, "A Profile of Baby Boomers at Mid-Decade." http://www.sba.gov/gopher/Business-Development/Success-Series/Vol10

Waller, Thomas "Fats," and Andy Razaf. FIND OUT WHAT THEY LIKE AND HOW THEY LIKE IT. Music by THOMAS "FATS" WALLER. Lyrics by ANDY RAZAF. © 1929 CHAPPELL & CO. Copyright Renewed. Rights for the Extended Term of Copyright in the U.S. assigned to CHAPPELL & CO. and RAZAF MUSIC CO. INC. All Rights Reserved. Used by Permission.

Wordsworth, William. "Lines Composed a Few Miles above Tintern Abbey," *William Wordsworth: Selected Poems and Prefaces.* Edited by Jack Stillinger. Boston: Houghton Mifflin Company, 1965.

# Index